A Helluva Life

A Helluva Life
As lived by
Helen Sprague Broomell

Sue Broomell Irujo

A HELLUVA LIFE:

AS LIVED BY HELEN SPRAGUE BROOMELL

All rights reserved.
Copyright © Suzanne Irujo, 2012

No part of this book may be reproduced or transmitted in any form or by any means, electronic or mechanical, including photocopying, recording, or by any information storage and retrieval system, without permission in writing from the author.

Cover drawing courtesy of Peggy Grinvalsky, used with permission;
cover design by Peggy Grinvalsky
Poem page 119 courtesy of Ron Broomell, used with permission

Photographs courtesy of:
Irujo/Barck family: pp. vii, 65, 97, 117, 118, 126
Camp Minocqua: pp. 3, 6, 37
Martha Winters (Leigh family): p. 10
Broomell family: pp. 12, 32, 49, 80, 92, 109
Clearwater Camp: p. 20
Minocqua Museum: p. 24
Beverly Plummer: pp. 59, 70

All photographs used with permission

Published by LinguaConcepts, Alexandria, NH
ISBN 978-1-105-78200-8

FOR HELEN

"THIS IS GETTING TO BE FUN."
(Helen Broomell)

Table of Contents

Introduction..x

Roots..1

Growing Up..9

Teenager...17

Young Mother 25

Return to the North Woods 37

Free at Last 53

A Tripping Grandmother....................75

Old Age..103

To My Yukon Loon Mom...................121

One Final Story.................................123

Timeline 125

Introduction

Acknowledgements

Note to the Reader

PEOPLE HAVE BEEN SUGGESTING FOR A LONG TIME THAT I write a book about my mother. I always thought having a book about Helen's life would be wonderful, but I didn't think I could write it. The idea wouldn't go away, though, so I began by writing a series of vignettes based on incidents I remembered and stories Helen and others had told. Those vignettes eventually became this book, but not without encouragement and contributions from many people.

Foremost among those who helped turn my musings into a book are my five siblings: Dare Broomell, Ken Broomell, Ron Broomell, Ann Broomell, and Jennie Gibson. Dare's wife Mary, besides contributing numerous memories of Helen, also graciously put up with my endless questions while I was writing. Three of Helen's best friends, Peggy Grinvalsky, Beverly Plummer, and Jim Stewart, gave me invaluable information. Greta Janssen, George DeMet, and Sue Ferguson made additional contributions, as did three of Helen's grandchildren. This book would not have been possible without all of them. A special thanks also goes to my friend, colleague, and editor *par excellence*, Lise Ragan, who very gently reminded me that readers outside the family would need additional information about dates, places, and events.

The book was never meant to be a full biography, but it took on a life of its own. The result is that it now somewhat resembles a biography, but has very few dates in it. Readers who expect to be reading a biography, and want to know exactly when and where all these things were happening, should consult the timeline beginning on page 125.

Much of what is recounted here came from stories told by friends and family, and it is in the nature of stories to change over time. If perhaps a few details have been elaborated (or exaggerated), the essence of the stories—and their depiction of Helen—remains true to who she was.

This book is first and foremost for Helen, my amazing mother. It is also for all those who contributed; for all Helen's large family of friends, relatives, and admirers; and for anybody wanting an example of how to live a full and joyful life, even in the face of adversity.

Sue Broomell Irujo

Roots

HELEN ADORED HER FATHER. JOHN PERLEY SPRAGUE WAS a handsome, rugged man, with a full head of white hair, intense blue eyes that twinkled when he laughed, and a wry sense of humor. He was known as Perley to his family when he was growing up; John to his friends and medical colleagues; Doctor or J. P. to his Camp Minocqua campers and counselors, and to Pottawattomie Lodge guests; and Gee Dee to his grandchildren. Nobody knows what Helen called him. He was a woodsman, a carpenter, an orthopedic surgeon, a storyteller, a canoeist, an avid tennis player into his seventies (unheard of at that time!), and a teacher and leader of young men. He knew how to stack shingles, trap bear, hunt moose, catch muskies, heal a wound, set a broken bone, and convey his love of nature to boys and young men. Helen loved the sweet smell of his pipe, his soft voice, his quiet demeanor, and especially the stories he told about his camping experiences and about the adventures he had when he first established Camp Minocqua.

Helen's daughter Ann, who never knew her grandfather because she was less than a year old when he died, looked at a portrait of him and called him "regal." (That same daughter, Ann, has somehow inherited an expression of her grandfather's—*hmm, hmm, hmm,* with each syllable falling on a lower tone. Can something like that be genetic?) I remember him as kind, soft-spoken, caring, gentle, mellow, and wise.

My older brother probably knew Gee Dee better than any of his other grandchildren did, since Dare was a camper at Camp Minocqua while our grandfather was still the camp director. Dare described him as "nonvolatile" because he never let anything bother him. My younger brother Ken remembers a good example of this. When he was a Camp Minocqua camper, he was out fishing in a small boat with several other campers, and one of them got a fishhook caught in his eyelid. The boys panicked, but they managed to get the boat to shore. Doctor put them all at ease, removed the fishhook, and gave the boy a rakish eyepatch, thus making him an instant celebrity. This was the manner in which Dr. Sprague dealt with whatever emergencies came up—calmly and without fuss (and there were bound to be many emergencies, with over 150 men and boys engaged in active camp activities). That calmness was one of the qualities, among many others, that John P. Sprague passed on to his daughter, Helen. In many ways, she was who she was largely due to her father's influence.

John Perley Sprague acquired his love of the outdoors early in life. He grew up in far northern Maine, and used to go with his father and grandfather on bear-trapping trips, where he learned to camp, fish, hunt, and trap. His

"HE WAS A MAN OF MANY SIDES,
AND GOOD ON EVERY SIDE."
(Dr. Hugh Elmer Brown, Dr. Sprague's pastor)

father had been a lumberman after the Civil War, and later built a sawmill and became a carpenter. In northern Maine during the last two decades of the nineteenth century, carpenters usually became undertakers as well, since they were the ones who made the caskets. And since carpenters also built tables and chairs, undertakers often owned furniture stores. So Ether Whitman Sprague, carpenter, undertaker, and Helen's grandfather (although she never knew him because he died before she was born), also had a furniture store. He was a civic-minded man who served as town treasurer for eight years, and in the Maine Legislature for two. His wife, Leonisa Estes Sprague, was a teacher and the first female Baptist minister ordained in the state of Maine. Helen's sense of contributing to one's community may have come from her grandfather, and her instinct to help others may have come from her grandmother.

John P. Sprague's early experiences had a great influence on his later life, and on Helen's. His chosen profession was medicine, and he made a great success of it: Professor of Hygiene and Sanitation, Professor of Orthopedic Surgery, Medical Officer during World War I, orthopedic surgeon in private practice. But he was a natural teacher, and his main interests were always the outdoors and fomenting love of the outdoors in boys and young men. While he was working as medical advisor and physical director for the Chicago Latin School for Boys, the headmaster suggested he start a boys' summer camp. Dr.

Sprague jumped at the opportunity.

The idea of starting a camp came during the very early years of the twentieth century. Those were busy years for John Perley Sprague. In a three-year time span, he graduated from medical school; married his college sweetheart, Mertie Belle Maxim; started Camp Minocqua by taking fourteen boys for a summer of fishing and wilderness camping on Bolger Lake in Minocqua, Wisconsin; welcomed his first daughter, Grace Maxim Sprague, into the world; and established Camp Minocqua in its permanent home on 65 acres of land he had purchased on Tomahawk Lake.

What a visionary Dr. Sprague must have been to invest in land in northern Wisconsin at that time! The whole area had been clear-cut, leaving only a few of the original towering Norway Pines around the lumber camps. The landscape was wretched, and the only access to what was to become the camp point was a tote road from the railway five miles away. Some of the early residents of Minocqua thought Dr. Sprague was foolish to buy acres and acres of land. In the early years of the twentieth century, the only value of the land was thought to be the trees on it, so why would anybody buy land with no trees?

In fact, there were more trees on the point of land Dr.

"ON WOODED SHORES OF TOMAHAWK,
WHERE GIANT PINES THEIR HEADS UPRAISE …"
(From the Camp Minocqua anthem)

Sprague bought for his camp than there were in most places in northern Wisconsin. The story goes that the wife of the lumber company boss was in charge of the lumber camp that had operated on that particular point of land on Tomahawk Lake in the late 1800s. She convinced her husband to leave more than just the two or three trees that were normally left standing around lumber camps. Those ten or twelve majestic old Norway Pines on the point later became emblems of Camp Minocqua, standing sentinel over that very special place, identifying the camp point from anywhere on the lake, and guiding tired campers back "home."

Dr. Sprague's vision was to provide wilderness experiences and character development for boys who would be the future leaders of their communities. The boys must have had a good time, because soon their parents were asking the good doctor if they could come to camp with their sons. So Dr. Sprague bought more land across the bay from Camp Minocqua, and established Pottawattomie Lodge, a resort for parents of the campers, friends of the parents, and anybody else who wanted to come. Whether it was the fresh air, the good fishing, the good food, the indoor plumbing (unknown in a rustic resort in those days), or the fact that the barren landscape was beginning to renew itself, Pottawattomie Lodge was a huge success.

Helen was born four years after Pottawattomie Lodge was established. The family lived in Evanston, Illinois, in the winter, and on Tomahawk Lake in the summer. Dr. Sprague continued purchasing land on the shores of Tomahawk Lake, and by 1924 he owned 240 acres, with two miles of shoreline. He sold pieces of it to friends, family members, and loyal camp counselors, who built summer cabins along the shores of the lake. Camp Minocqua, Pottawattomie Lodge, and friendly neighbors—this was the environment in which Helen spent the summers of her growing-up years.

Growing Up

DR. SPRAGUE'S DAUGHTER HELEN WAS ONE OF THE MOST popular "guests" at Pottawattomie Lodge when she was very young. With shining reddish-blonde hair and the face of an impish angel, she got even more attention and compliments than the excellent food served in the Lodge dining room. Helen made her first appearance at the Lodge when she was six months old, and returned every summer as she was growing up. Many of the guests also returned to the Lodge year after year, and they watched her grow from an infant into a coquettish toddler who charmed her way into getting anything she wanted. Later, they watched her mature into one of those little girls who is "six going on sixteen." She was a fixture at Pottawattomie Lodge, looked after by her older sister Grace while their parents were busy running the Lodge and Camp Minocqua.

Helen had a wonderful imagination as a very young child. When there was extra space at the Lodge, she stayed in one of the cabins, pretending she was a guest. But her favorite flight of imagination was the creation of a fairy garden on the shore of Tomahawk Lake. The fairies "were a very important part of my growing-up years," as she retold it over seventy years later. The garden had to be

"THE FAIRIES COULD GO FROM THEIR DINING ROOM TO THEIR SWIMMING AREA."

(Helen, speaking of her fairy gardens on the shoreline of Pottawattomie Lodge in the early 1920s)

right on the lakeshore because "the important thing was that the fairies could go from their dining room to their swimming area." She picked a nice flat area under the trees, and cleared away sticks and pine cones so the fairies would have a place to dance. Helen would leave acorn caps in the "dining room," filled with a beautiful red liquid that her mother assured her was the fairies' favorite food. In the morning, the red liquid would be gone and a small gift left in its place. It wasn't until many years later that Helen discovered the red liquid was Lavoris mouthwash, and it was the Pottawattomie Lodge guests who took turns leaving small gifts for her.

Much later in her life, when her two younger daughters

were little girls, Helen helped them make fairy gardens on the hillside behind their house on Tomahawk Lake.

As Helen grew a little older, she began to notice that her father wasn't around much during the summer. When she asked where he was, she was told he was "at camp." Helen thought she should be able to go to camp, too. She understood that Camp Minocqua was a boys' camp, but she didn't understand why she couldn't be a boy if she wanted to. She thought being a boy meant doing all the things boys did. She could run fast, and swim, and play baseball. Helen even joined a boys' sandlot baseball team in Evanston, where her family lived in the winter, to show her father that she was just as good as any boy. As she said years later, "I went to all kinds of crazy antics just to show my father that I'd be a very good boy, and I'd like to go to Camp Minocqua." The antics didn't help get her into Camp Minocqua, however, and a few years later, when she was sent to Camp Warwick Woods—for girls— she had to accept the fact that she would never be a boy.

Helen continued to be spoiled by the Pottawattomie Lodge guests even after she grew out of the cute little girl stage. Her mother had been in poor health most of Helen's life, her father was busy with the boys' camp, and her teenaged sister had interests of her own. So the guests took it upon themselves to watch over Helen, which

THE "BELLE" OF POTTAWATTOMIE LODGE, AGE 6
*(Painted by Elizabeth K. Peyraud, well-known
Chicago artist of the early 20th century)*

involved lots of presents and letting her do anything she wanted to. It was worse after Helen's mother died. Helen was eleven, and her older sister Grace was already married. Her father had never been very involved in Helen's upbringing, and after his wife died, he hired a series of housekeepers to look after his daughter. Most of them were more interested in snagging the handsome, eligible doctor than they were in taking care of his daughter. This resulted in more presents, and more getting her own way. Years later, reminiscing about her early life, Helen said, "I missed having a mother. I didn't feel it then, but when I grew older, I realized that some of my problems came from the fact that there wasn't a mother figure in our house." This was one of the few times Helen ever admitted she had any problems at all in her life.

Helen wasn't really born in a canoe, although it may have sometimes seemed that way. Her earliest memories included her father going off with the older campers on weeks-long wilderness canoe trips, and her mother paddling along the shores of beautiful Tomahawk Lake with Pottawattomie Lodge guests. Helen was not allowed to go out in a canoe until she proved she was a strong swimmer. When she had done that, she gloried in paddling by herself around the Pottawattomie Lodge bay, and during the summers spent most of her time on or in the lake—she loved to swim almost as much as she loved canoeing.

A couple of years after her mother died, Helen was involved in a canoeing incident, which later became one of her favorite stories. She "thought it would be a delightful thing to sleep in a canoe," as she put it, so she got permission from her father, chose a night with a bright full moon, put blanket and pillow in the canoe, and set off paddling. The gentle breeze that was blowing her toward the middle of the lake soon turned into a much stronger wind. Helen decided to go back to the Lodge, but found she couldn't paddle against the ever-increasing wind. So with the canoe being blown more than paddled, she steered a course to a beach on the other side of the lake, where she knew there was a trail back to the Lodge. She reached the far shore, pulled the canoe up as far as she could on the beach—which wasn't really very far, since this was a full-size, heavy, wood and canvas canoe—turned it over and put the paddle under it, found the trail, and started back to the Lodge.

In the meantime, her father had decided to go and get her in a small motorboat. He found the canoe on the beach where Helen had left it, looking like it had blown up on the sand, and of course feared the worst. Going quickly back to the Lodge, he enlisted the help of the guests to search for Helen. In her words, "There was pandemonium at that whole end of the lake" as the Lodge guests spread out across the water in canoes and rowboats, calling out for Helen.

On her return to the Lodge, Helen insisted she had never been lost—*she* knew where she was all the time. But she accepted her father's decision that she not be allowed to use the canoes for the rest of the summer, and later claimed that she "never did quite so foolish a thing again"—a debatable statement for anybody who knows of the wonderfully foolish adventures she embarked on late in her life.

Teenager

HELEN WAS A CHARMER AS SHE MOVED INTO HER TEENAGE years. She was cute, bright, vivacious, and athletic, with curly reddish hair, and she loved talking with anybody she met (a trait she maintained throughout her life). That tendency to talk with anybody almost got Helen in trouble when she was in her early teens. She was riding a streetcar home, in Evanston, and had gotten into a conversation with a fellow passenger, who just happened to be a man of an age that young girls probably shouldn't be talking with on streetcars. But Helen didn't notice that, and she had no fear of strangers. To her, any person was a good person (another trait she maintained throughout her life). When her streetcar stop came, she said goodbye to the man, got off, walked home, and sat down on the back porch to wait for her father to return home. She hadn't noticed that the man had also gotten off the streetcar and followed her, until he suddenly appeared on the porch and began kissing her. Just at that moment, Helen's father pulled into the driveway and the man ran away, unseen by Dr. Sprague. Helen never told her father about the incident, but many years later described it to friends as "interesting."

Perhaps Helen's early and abiding interest in the opposite sex sprang from a desire to know what came after the kissing. We don't know when she actually found out the facts of life. She once said that her father's discussion of the "birds and bees" was too literally about birds and bees to be useful. In her words, "My father was very shy about it, he just didn't call a spade a spade. He had to make it a little more presentable." Helen said her father asked her older sister Grace to explain to her "where babies come from, and so forth and so forth, because I just got snips and snatches from classmates, when we'd gather up in a corner of the playground and ask questions of one another, but never getting anywhere." We don't know how old Helen was when that explanation was finally forthcoming.

All of Helen's canoeing experience as a child at Pottawattomie Lodge ended up paying off. At age thirteen, and in her second year as a camper at the Holiday Camps in Minnesota, she was chosen to go on their Canadian canoe trip, with girls who were all two years older than she was. It was a great honor, but what was more important to her, it was the fulfillment of her childhood dream of going on a wilderness canoe trip. Of course, Helen's dream had always been to go with her father, but this was the next best thing, and she was hooked on canoe tripping for life.

Attending the Holiday Camps had another huge effect on Helen's life: her father fell in love with Halokwe, the owner and director of the camps. Sara Gregg Holiday had chosen the name Halokwe fifteen years previously, when she first joined the group of people who organized the Camp Fire Girls. (According to her journal, Sara—or Sadie, as she was then known—thought the name Halokwe meant "ant god of healing, perseverance, etc." but it appears to be the Zuni Indian name for their "ant fraternity," a group of men who performed ceremonial songs and dances to ants, believed by the Zuni to cause disease.) Halokwe was an independent woman in her late forties who had never married—she had been too busy helping organize the Camp Fire Girls and then starting her own private girls' camp. There were bound to be clashes between her and Helen, as they were two very independent women of very different ages who both loved the same man. So Helen decided to go to boarding school in Mississippi. She claimed she went away in order to give her father and Halokwe "a little more time for themselves," in her words—but the fact is her decision was probably influenced more by being able to swim all winter at the school.

While at school in Mississippi, Helen received a visit from her father and Halokwe, who had taken the train all the way from Chicago to Mississippi to ask Helen's permission to marry. John Perley Sprague and Sara Gregg Holiday were married in Hackensack, Minnesota the following fall.

Her father's marriage to Halokwe shortly after Helen returned from her school year away necessarily involved

"SOMEONE OLDER WAS ALWAYS
WITH ME ON CANOE TRIPS."
(Helen as a very young counselor at Clearwater Camp)

quite a few adjustments. Some friction was unavoidable, what with Helen's natural independence and the freedom she had while growing up, plus having had her father to herself for four years. "We had to get together and see if we could respect one another's viewpoints, but problems were inevitable," Helen related years later—although she never elaborated on what kinds of problems they were.

Whatever problems there might have been in getting along at home, Helen's new stepmother respected her experience and enthusiasm in the areas of canoeing and camping. The Holiday Camps had been sold when Halokwe married Dr. Sprague, and together they established a new girls' camp in Minocqua. Clearwater Camp was set up on rented land on Clear Lake, not far from Tomahawk Lake. At age sixteen, Helen became the youngest counselor on the staff of the new girls' camp, and acquired the camp name Spraggles. She was given a lot of responsibility for planning and supervising canoe trips, even at such a young age. Helen later insisted she had always explained to people that an older counselor was along on all her trips, but it's more likely that she tried to pass herself off as older than sixteen.

Dr. Sprague's remarriage brought about other changes as well. The same year Clearwater Camp was established, a large, beautiful log edifice, which Doctor and Halokwe named the Anchor, was built on a point of land between Camp Minocqua and Pottawattomie Lodge. The building was combination home, office, and Pottawattomie Lodge space. The basement included a recreation room, a tearoom, and an immense kitchen with a dumb waiter connecting to the upstairs kitchen. (In reality, the basement kitchen was exactly the same size and shape as the upstairs kitchen, which was certainly not "immense," but I remember it as being immense when I was a child.) Upstairs at the Anchor there was family living space, office space, and two rental rooms, which supplemented the various cabins that provided sleeping space for Lodge guests. Helen would often sit in the tearoom imagining herself having tea (or cocktails?) with exotic men in exotic places.

Even though the Anchor was built as a year-round home, Dr. Sprague and Halokwe still spent winters in Evanston, and Helen attended Evanston High School. One year, however, the family stayed at the Anchor all winter. Helen loved the winter she spent in Minocqua. She delighted in the beauty of the snowy pines and birch trees, which were regrowing into a beautiful forest after the clear-cutting of the late nineteenth century. She enjoyed going to high school in Minocqua, where one small brick building housed grades one through twelve. Her father's attention was focused more on his new wife than on his daughter, and Helen's new stepmother never did take on the role of mother, so Helen enjoyed a delightful winter of being able to do very much whatever she chose.

Not that Helen ever did anything *really* bad. But her cousin Bud Sprague, who with his parents was also spending the winter in Minocqua that year, thought she was always misbehaving. He almost seemed afraid of her, and didn't want to go places with her because she was so "wild." What was wild to Bud may have been normal to Helen, though. Although he was a year older than she was, Helen was by far the more outgoing, adventuresome, and risk-taking of the two. Bud was quiet, shy, and studious. Helen was more interested in high school boys than in high school studies, and wasn't afraid to take a drink if she could get one.

After high school, Helen spent a year at Stephens College in Columbia, Missouri, and then became a sorority girl at Northwestern University in Evanston. During the summers she continued as a counselor at Clearwater, which is how she met Jack Broomell. His parents had been guests at Pottawattomie Lodge, and Jack was a counselor at Camp Minocqua. Helen easily fell in love with this handsome, charming, brooding young man, and dropped out of college to marry him. She was twenty years old.

I asked my mother later in life why she never went back to school to finish her degree. Her response was typical of her: "Why? So I could teach physical education in the state of Illinois?"

"Could this be Helen's wedding picture?"
(Greta Janssen, friend and photograph archivist)

Young Mother

Helen loved being pregnant, and loved being a mother even more. Nursing her first son Dare, rocking slowly, daydreaming of what he would be when he grew up: What peaceful times those were. She could put her little worries out of her mind—her husband's tendency to drink too much, her mother-in-law's coolness toward her —and bask in the joys of motherhood.

There were fewer peaceful moments after I arrived, what with Dare being only a little over a year old when I was born. And Jack's mother grew ever more distant. Helen wondered why she couldn't make a connection with her mother-in-law. Was it because she hadn't finished college? Was it her lack of housekeeping skills? Or simply a mother's belief that no woman was good enough for her son? Helen had always enjoyed her father's approval, and didn't know how to deal with Mother Broomell's silent disapproval. When I was less than a week old, Helen's musings took the form of a note and poem written by her new baby girl to her grandmother:

Dear Grandma —

You may think that this is a bit unconventional for me to be writing a letter at the delicate age of six days. However, I want you all to understand that I mean to make good use of this excellent mind which my father so generously bestowed upon me. As yet, a pencil seems a bit unwieldy, so I took the liberty of dictating this to my mamma this morning at two.

A Helluva Life

Following in the steps of my famed Aunt Muffy, I composed a poem, and herewith submit same for your approval or disapproval as the case may be. Remember, though — I'm a little young to take any very deriding criticism.

≈≈ To Grandma ≈≈

I have a button for a nose
And ten tiny nails on ten tiny toes,
In fact I seem to be replete
With all I need from head to feet.
Just wait till I'm out from under this glass,
You'll see I'm rather a pretty lass.
I scream with vim,
Then eat with vigor,
In order to keep
My girlish figure.
My mamma even says I'm rude
The way I try to bolt my food.
Perhaps she's wrong – perhaps she's right,
But I won't give in without a fight.
* * *
And here it is my grandma's birthday —
Why must I be so far away?
However, I think if she'll do her part,
I'll find my way to my grandma's heart,
And there I'll stay
Forever and a day —
Held safe in my grandma's heart.
Lovingly,

Suzanne

Young Mother

Reading between the lines, it almost seems that Helen had given up on winning over her mother-in-law, but hoped her beautiful newborn daughter would be able to do so. Unfortunately, it was never to be, for either Helen or for me. Jack's mother had a stroke when I was very young, and lived the rest of her life partially paralyzed—a bitter, querulous, demanding old woman.

(I suspect Helen got cold feet about sending this letter. If she had sent it, the poem would never have come into my possession. She must have kept it for some reason, and its preservation through three moves shows that it was very meaningful to her.)

Helen was also a bit troubled by the fact that she didn't see as much of her father as she would like to. She lived on the north side of Chicago, and he lived in Evanston, so they were not very far apart. She tried not to let it bother her; after all, he had a new wife to take care of, and Helen had a new husband to take care of her. Besides, there were now two camps and a resort to run. But she missed his kindness, his understanding, and his twinkling smile.

Jack had a good job in the accounting department of a publishing company in Chicago, and the family was soon able to move out of the city. Helen delighted in the little rented house on a quiet street in Park Ridge. It had two small squares of grass in front and a larger, sloping, fenced-in yard in back, with garden space around the edges. (Helen was never much for gardening, but she did plant a Victory Garden during the war—a few packets of carrot seeds thrown into the garden beds.) She loved to stand on the back porch and watch her two children rolling down the grassy slope. They would laugh constantly as they went down, then pick themselves up, run back up the hill, and laugh their way down again, and again, and again. What pleasure her children gave her! She spent a lot of time with them, baking cookies, doing art projects, reading Winnie the Pooh stories and poems from *When We Were Very Young* and *Now We Are Six*. (I still have the four-volume set of A. A. Milne poetry and Winnie the Pooh books that my mother gave me on my sixth birthday.)

Helen's marriage gave her less pleasure. She hadn't known Jack's social drinking would turn into daily drinking, or that drinking exacerbated his moodiness. But she didn't dwell on that. It was not in her nature to dwell on anything unpleasant.

It was in Park Ridge that Helen began an ongoing Christmas tradition. Dare and I were to see no indication that Christmas was coming until Christmas morning.

Young Mother

There were no decorations or gifts visible anywhere in the house. An unused room on the first floor, with curtained French doors, was kept closed during the weeks before Christmas. When we came downstairs on Christmas morning, the open doors disclosed a beautifully decorated Christmas tree surrounded by piles of presents. Of course, as we grew older, Dare and I remembered previous Christmases, but everybody pretended we didn't know what was happening behind those closed doors.

Later, in other houses, it was more difficult to maintain the tradition because there was never again a special room that could be closed off for weeks before Christmas. But the tradition of not seeing the Christmas tree until Christmas morning continued, which meant that the tree couldn't be put up and decorated until the children were in bed. With an impatient, intolerant husband who could never stop at one or two drinks while trimming the tree, that was a recipe for disaster. So as Dare and I grew older, we were allowed to stay up and help after our two little brothers had gone to bed on Christmas Eve. And when Ken and Ron grew older, they did the same for their two little sisters.

Even after all her children were old enough to stay up and help decorate the tree on Christmas Eve, Helen continued surprising everybody. After her father's handmade mahogany canoe had found a permanent home hanging from the ceiling of her living room, Helen would cut a big Christmas tree, put it directly under the canoe, and then cut the top off and put it on top of the canoe. It looked exactly as if the canoe had been cut in half.

Dare and I share another memory from Park Ridge—one that shows the hypocrisy of our father's behavior throughout his marriage. Jack's younger brother Frank had returned from the World War II European war theater, where he had served his country valiantly, and was paying our family a visit. Perhaps it was his bravery in the war that enabled him to find the courage to disclose to his older brother that he was gay—a very difficult thing to do in the 1940s. Instead of praising Frank for his war service and accepting his homosexuality, Jack berated him, telling Frank in no uncertain terms that he was not welcome in our house. Uncle Frank's name could never again be mentioned in Jack's presence. And while Jack continued getting drunk frequently, verbally abusing his wife, and seeing other women, Frank went on to develop a committed relationship with a lifelong partner.

Helen made up for Jack's injustice years later, after she divorced him. It may have been out of a sense of guilt over Jack's unfair treatment of Frank, or more likely due to her innate interest in and acceptance of every human being—whatever the reason, she visited

Frank in New York City during one of her trips east. A deep friendship developed between them, lasting over 25 years, until Helen's death. Helen visited Frank every time she got anywhere near New York City, and Frank called her often for long phone conversations. After Helen's death, Frank continued those phone calls with Dare's wife Mary, and later with me as well, calling us every Christmas season until his death.

There was one theme that was to be recurrent throughout Helen's marriage: the tension between the independence she had developed during her growing-up years and her husband's need to keep her subservient. That tension was just beginning to develop during the early years of her marriage, and World War II gave her an opportunity to keep it at bay for a while. With the factories running full blast to produce war matériel, and so many men away at war, housewives were put to work on the factory lines. Working in one of those factories for a few years gave Helen the opportunity to satisfy her need for independence. She looked just like the poster of "Rosie the Riveter," with a twinkle in her eye and her auburn hair in two long braids crisscrossed over the top of her head and covered with a kerchief. Her part-time night work, and the money it brought in, gave Helen a feeling of being useful, even though everything she

"Wow! She was a glamour girl!"
(Sue's reaction on seeing this picture for the first time)

earned went directly into the household pot.

When Helen exchanged her riveter's kerchief and coveralls for a stylish skirt and blouse or dress, and coiled her braids into spirals on either side of her head, she turned heads when she walked down the street. I always remembered the braids and the sweet smile, but never realized how glamorous my mother really was until a photograph of her that I had never seen before turned up years later. My reaction was "Wow!"

After a couple of years in Park Ridge, Jack and Helen moved to Elgin, Illinois. Jack was on his best behavior as he began a new job, and both Dare and I were in school. Helen felt free, happy, and creative. She had the time and the inclination to indulge her love of painting, drawing, and crafts: watercolors, pencil, ink; landscapes, people, still lifes; linoleum blocks, candle making, paper creations. She enrolled in a painting class at the local Art Institute, and enrolled Dare and me in ceramics classes. Helen painted beautiful watercolors, but the clay pieces Dare and I made embarrassed us whenever she showed them off to friends or relatives—something she did well into our teenage years. Helen gave me an oil painting set for Christmas when I was about eight years old, complete with easel and palette, but my one attempt at "Still Life With Blocks" discouraged me from ever trying again, and my mother didn't push it. We did many craft projects together, however, making candles, linoleum block prints, Halloween costumes, Christmas cards, and much more. Those were happy days for all of us, but they didn't last very long.

Over time, Jack was becoming increasingly difficult to live with. As his drinking escalated, his tendency to blame Helen for anything that went wrong also escalated. She was subjected to growing amounts of verbal abuse, and occasionally became the target of hurled objects (although they always missed). Jack's participation in family activities dwindled to almost nothing. The only thing he was willing to do was visit his mother and older sister Muffy, who lived in a suburb of Chicago, but those visits always ended up in arguments with his sister and with Helen about the care of his mother, partially paralyzed by a stroke.

Even as Helen was being forced more and more firmly under Jack's thumb, she always found little ways of asserting her independent streak. What other 1940s suburban housewife would catch a baby skunk when it was still too young to produce a stink, have its stinker removed, and make a pet out of it? That skunk followed Helen around the house for several years.

Summers in Minocqua were a godsend. Clearwater Camp

had been moved to the former site of Pottawattomie Lodge, which now operated, on a much-reduced scale, out of the Anchor and a few cabins. Jack returned to Camp Minocqua as a counselor a few times during the early- and mid-forties, so the whole family spent those summers on Tomahawk Lake. Once Dare and I were old enough to be campers, Helen was able to again be a counselor at Clearwater. Jack never drank as much during summers in Minocqua as he did at other times, so any summer the family spent in Minocqua was a happy one for Helen. No matter how much she tried to make the most of her suburban housewife life, Helen had been raised on the shores of Tomahawk Lake, and she was always happiest when she was either in the lake or on it.

Another thing that made Helen happy during the summers she spent in Minocqua was that she was able to see more of her father. During the fall, winter, and spring months, Jack was occupied with his own demons, Helen was busy with her children, and her father and Halokwe were totally involved with the two camps and with American Camping Association activities. The two families didn't see much of each other, even though they lived only about 40 miles apart. In the summer, however, there was always time for leisurely chats on one or the other of the camp office porches after camp activities were finished for the day.

During her pregnancy with her third child, Ken, Helen

was alone in Minocqua for most of the summer. Dare and I were both in camp, and Jack had to stay in Elgin to work, so he was there only on weekends. Helen stayed in one of the old Pottawattomie Lodge cabins that stood on a hill overlooking Clearwater Camp and the lake. She gloried in the solitude, which may have been what first gave her the idea of canoeing in Alaska. A few years before that, a man named Slim Williams had been a counselor at Camp Minocqua. Slim had spent years exploring the Alaskan wilderness by dog sled, and was a wonderful story teller, mesmerizing his listeners with tales of wondrous adventures, told in his soft, gravelly voice. Helen had spent many hours sitting around a campfire listening to those stories, and later acknowledged that she chose Alaska for her late-life adventures largely because of Slim's influence.

During the four years the family lived in Elgin, Jack's drinking worsened to the point that his job was in danger because of it. At the same time, Dr. Sprague was thinking about retiring as director of Camp Minocqua. If things could be arranged between her husband and her father, Helen might be able to move back to her beloved "wooded shores of Tomahawk" (a phrase from the first line of the Camp Minocqua anthem).

Return to the North Woods

OH, THE EXCITEMENT OF IT ALL! HELEN AND HER FAMILY were moving to Minocqua. Jack was about to lose his job as comptroller of a publishing company in Elgin at the same time that Dr. Sprague was ready to turn Camp Minocqua over to somebody else. And a charming two-bedroom lake cabin was available at a price they could manage. The cabin already felt like it was in the family, since Jack and Helen were buying it from the father-in-law of Helen's older sister, Grace Sprague Cameron.

CAMP MINOCQUA IN 1948
(When Helen finally got to "go to the boys' camp")

So in the early summer of 1948, Helen and Jack put their furniture in storage, gathered their four children, and moved to Minocqua. Dare and I were in grade school, Ken was a toddler of two, and Ron was less than six months old. That first summer in Minocqua was no different than previous summers spent on Tomahawk Lake had been. The family stayed in one of the former Pottawattomie Lodge cabins, and the two older children were in camp. Helen looked after the two younger ones, and Jack helped run Camp Minocqua. Fall came, and the renovations on the Cameron cabin to make it into a year-round home were not yet finished, so the family moved into the second floor of the original Pottawattomie Lodge building, which now housed Clearwater Camp offices on the first floor and had rooms for kitchen help on the second floor. It looked and felt like an old hotel, which is exactly what it had been, but it was the only available building with heat and room for six people. Although far from warm and cozy, it was adequate for the winter. After so many summers spent at Pottawattomie Lodge and Clearwater Camp, Helen felt like she was back home.

Disaster almost struck the first year after the family's return to Minocqua. Part of running a camp meant doing a promotional trip, so Jack and Helen set off for the Chicago area in mid-March, planning to be gone for about six weeks. They left the children in the care of Granny Brown, a competent woman who lived nearby and moved in with us for the time our parents were gone.

April came, and with it ice-out. Dare and Ken were outside one windy day playing with a volleyball on the Clearwater Camp tennis court. The tennis court was right next to the lake, and when a gust of wind blew the ball into the lake, Dare got a canoe and went after it. In the meantime, two-year-old Ken, who had wanted to go in the canoe with Dare, decided to walk into the water after him. The lake had been ice-covered only a day or two earlier, and Ken collapsed from the cold. Dare saw what had happened, and turned back immediately, but no eleven-year-old boy paddling a large two-person canoe against a strong wind was going to make it back to shore very quickly.

The couple of minutes it took Dare to get to where Ken was and drag him out of the water must have seemed like an eternity to him. He immediately started artificial respiration, which he had learned at camp the previous summer. In the meantime, Granny Brown had seen it all and called her grandson, who lived nearby. Ken was rushed to the local doctor in Minocqua, who took one look at him and said, "There's nothing I can do for him; if you can get him to the hospital in Rhinelander fast enough, maybe he'll live." That thirty-mile trip to the hospital must have been the fastest anybody had ever made at that time. It all happened so fast that there wasn't even time to call Jack and Helen, who knew nothing about it until after Ken had been treated and was out of danger. Had Helen known immediately after it happened, she would have thought about it for a moment and said, "Of course he'll be all right." Had Jack known, he would have ranted and raved about careless brothers and incompetent caretakers. Jack often ranted and raved about things that were not accurate. In this case, Dare's administration of artificial respiration, Granny Brown's quick phone call, and her grandson's heroic rush to the hospital had saved Ken's life.

It didn't happen all at once, and Helen wasn't really aware of it at the time, but after moving to Minocqua, she finally achieved her childhood dream of "going to the boys' camp." At first, nothing was different except that the family didn't have to go back to Illinois at the end of the summer. Helen took care of her four children, and reveled in having a house of her own, turning it from a rustic summer cabin into a uniquely decorated year-round home. Dare and I were always aware that our house didn't look anything like our friends' houses. The living room furniture was Danish modern (unknown in Minocqua in the early 1950s); a very old and very large authentic Polynesian tapa cloth with an intricate geometric design hung on one of the living room walls; and Helen's handpainted picture maps of the two camps covered the doors of the kitchen closets. Other things weren't as obvious to us then, but as Dare said later, "The whole wall of books was more different than we realized at the time." (Jack was a life-time member of the Book-of-the-Month club. He read all the books cover to cover as soon as he received them, and saved them all. Helen's taste in books ran more to offbeat poetry and books about nature and wilderness than to Book-of-the-Month club selections.)

Jack gradually took over more of the responsibility for running the camp. But being self-employed was not a good alternative for a man who had very little self-control, and Helen ended up doing much of the work for him, while he drank or snored on the sofa. He made all the decisions, however, and in spite of her confidence and independent spirit, Helen had to fight to keep herself from internalizing Jack's belief that she was capable of nothing other than housework and secretarial work. The truth is that Helen was never very big on housework, but she was very good at secretarial work. She gradually took over the camp office from the elderly camp secretary who had been with her father for years. During camp sessions, there was always a counselor's wife with young children who was more than happy to look after Helen's two young boys along with her own children, so Helen could run the office. Ken and Ron later became campers themselves—at an earlier age than boys who were not sons of the camp director.

Helen's openness and caring about other people began to blossom as she interacted with campers, parents, counselors, and visitors. She took care of everybody who walked through the office door, no matter what they wanted, always putting other people's needs ahead of the need to get a list or a letter typed up—even if it meant later having to skip lunch or dinner to get the typing done on time. She established wonderful relationships with the campers, and lived their achievements and disappointments as vividly as if they had been her own.

Not that she didn't have achievements of her own, in addition to her capable work and smiling presence in the camp office. Helen thoroughly enjoyed participating in the annual camp water show, in which campers and counselors demonstrated their aquatic skills, and the campers and counselors thoroughly enjoyed watching her participate. At first it was just diving—she had always been an excellent diver, with jackknives and back flips executed in perfect form. Later she began entering the waterfront area by gunneling a canoe, to the cheers of the assembled audience. (Gunneling is the fine art of standing up in the stern of a canoe, balanced on the gunnels, which are the wooden or metal strips on top of the sides of a canoe, and propelling the canoe forward by bouncing up and down.) When the camp introduced various forms of towing people behind motor boats—aquaplaning, saucering, and later water skiing—Helen became the star of the show by standing on her head on an aquaplane or saucer. One year, when there were enough able and willing women around the camp, she even organized a chorus line that danced the cancan on the swim raft.

Helen never did any of this to get attention—she was just having fun—but nobody could say she didn't enjoy the attention she got.

Another thing Helen enjoyed was being with her father more. Dr. Sprague continued to co-direct the camp with Jack for a few years, so Helen saw a lot of him during the first summers after she returned to Minocqua. Even after retiring completely as director, he continued as camp physician, and was always at the head table in the dining room for meals. And he still loved to sit on the old rustic wooden chairs on the porch of the office, overlooking the camp bay and sheltered by the huge branches of the original Norway pines, telling stories from his past.

Gradually Dr. Sprague came to spend less time at the camp, and more time at the Anchor. And, of course, there eventually came a year when he was no longer there. John Perley Sprague died peacefully and easily, at age 86, only a day or two after experiencing a stroke. It was a life well lived.

Because of Jack's drinking, there was never much money in the household. The children weren't aware of that, however. Jack had never reconciled himself to the fact that his parents no longer had money after the stock market crash in 1929, and he did everything he could, including amassing a good deal of debt, to maintain an appearance of prosperity. Helen never cared about money for its own sake, but she was acutely aware that she never had a penny of her own to spend on little things she might want. So she hatched several different moneymaking schemes over the years. The acquisition of a pair of purebred but undocumented Siamese cats was supposed to be the beginning of a breeding business. Although she may have sold a few kittens, the most obvious result was simply too many cats around the house all the time. After making a mosaic table for herself that turned out beautifully, Helen decided that making more mosaic tables might be a good way to bring in some extra cash. But snipping tiles was a messy business, and a variety of art projects is always more satisfying than repeating the same one over and over, so that too went by the wayside.

Art continued to be a very important part of her life, and the lack of money forced Helen to find inexpensive outlets for her creative urges. She had once bought a small palm sander for one of her projects, and Jack went through the roof when he found out she had spent twenty dollars on herself. Because she had long since learned that preventing his outbursts made life much easier than dealing with them, she became a specialist in creating low-cost art. One such project started with a large piece of styrofoam, which she stuck in a snow bank and took a blowtorch to, then sprayed with copper paint and enhanced with coils of copper wire. Voilà: instant, inexpensive art. Over the years, her house came to look increasingly like a museum, what with her own works and many pieces given to her by artist friends.

Helen's two younger boys were now the beneficiaries of her love of art and literature. Just as I have very fond memories of ceramics and candle making with my mother, Ron also remembers always having some sort of art project in the works. The books of choice for reading aloud with Ken and Ron were not only *Winnie the Pooh*, A. A. Milne's poetry, and *A Child's Garden of Verses*, as Dare and I remember so well, but also beatnik poets and *The Prophet*. Whether it was his early exposure to beatnik poetry, or the fact that he had inherited fewer of Jack's inhibitions and more of Helen's independence, Ron grew up to be a poet, musician, artist, and permanent hippie.

Besides her love of people and art projects, Helen also

demonstrated a great love of everything in nature, including animals. There were always a dog and several cats in the house, which is, of course, hardly worth commenting on. Nor is feeding birds and squirrels, or keeping rabbits in the backyard. But how many people make pets out of skunks and raccoons? Yes, there was another pet skunk during those years. And there were two pet raccoon projects: One didn't work because the raccoon was not young enough when caught, and could only be handled with very thick gloves. Helen gave up on that one. The other was so successful that I was able to take it with me when I went out bar-hopping. Walking into a beer bar with a live raccoon around your neck is sure to attract some young man's attention.

One spring Helen came across a very young fawn whose mother was nowhere to be seen. She watched for several days, and when there was no sign of a mother, Helen contacted the Department of Natural Resources and received permission to feed the fawn and keep it at the camp through the summer. It grew accustomed to having people around all the time, and when the campers went home, it started following Helen around constantly, even into the house, to her immense surprise and pleasure.

Years passed, and Helen's marriage continued to deteriorate, but in spite of everything, she always had a positive attitude toward life. She never got rattled about anything, and developed amazing coping mechanisms. Jack had a succession of girl friends, which she ignored. He had no office to go to and no specific work hours, so he was always there to complain about everything she did, but Helen never confronted him about the way he treated her. He verbally abused her by keeping her up at night for hours on end, berating her about unimportant things she did, or the children did, that bothered him. Every time that happened, Helen suffered through it silently, and usually managed to take a nap the next day. She had four wonderful children, and she enjoyed living in Minocqua and working at the camp. Life went on.

The contradiction between Helen's independence and her subservience during her marriage is hard to understand. She would do anything to please Jack, and never stood up to him or complained about his unfair treatment or the miserable situation he created for her and their children. But at the same time, she was somehow able to sustain the self-confidence she had developed as a child and a teenager, which helped her survive, and even thrive, during those difficult years. The submissiveness was certainly not internalized; it was probably just easier to keep the calm than to deal with the results of rocking the boat. Whatever the reason, Helen somehow managed to keep her essential qualities of independence, creativity, and *joie de vivre* all through her marriage to Jack.

Helen remained as beautiful as ever during those years.

She cut her hair short—after all, she was a working mother now, and didn't have time to fuss with braids. Perhaps her eyes twinkled a little less, and her smile may have been a little forced, but her love of life could not be suppressed.

One year, when she was old enough so she should have been through with child bearing, Helen found herself pregnant again. She later claimed she got pregnant on purpose to see if another child would improve her marriage. If that was true, she should have known better. Ann's birth seemed to make Jack happier for a while. This beautiful little girl, who was born more than twenty years after his first little girl, became the apple of his eye. But that didn't change his drinking, or his behavior toward Helen.

Three years after Ann was born, Helen suspected she was pregnant again. On consulting her obstetrician, he informed her that it must be a "psychological pregnancy" because she was too old to become pregnant. A couple of months later she went back and told the obstetrician that her "psychological pregnancy was kicking." Jennie's birth, however, made even less difference in Jack's behavior than Ann's birth had.

There were always art projects and books around while Ann and Jennie were young, just as there had been with Dare and me, and later with Ken and Ron.

"THE WORLD ALWAYS LOOKS BRIGHTER
FROM BEHIND A SMILE."
(Quote from an unknown source)

The literature of choice for reading aloud during those years was *The Hobbit*. The art projects were one of Jennie's favorite parts of growing up. She loved the fact that her mother "made art out of things other people would say was junk." After Helen was divorced and Ann had gone off to college, Jennie was the only child left at home, and she won a scholarship to go to a private boarding school for a year. Helen's comment about having the house to herself was: "Now I don't have to clean up after myself in order to set the table for dinner."

Helen had missed canoe tripping all during her marriage, and as the years went on, she decided there was no reason not to be doing something she loved so much. So one year, spontaneous as always, she decided it was time for her to go on a Canadian canoe trip. Camp was over for the summer, and the campers and most of the counselors had departed. Her youngest son, Ron, and a few of the "old faithful" counselors were still around, sleeping in one of the cabins and helping put the camp to bed for the winter. One morning Helen appeared in the cabin while they were all still asleep, exclaiming, "Wake up! We're going to Canada!" Nobody, not even Helen herself, knew about the trip ahead of time, but they got everything packed up, and Helen, four young men, and the camp caretaker, Don—who was a close friend of Jack and Helen's, as well as a valued camp employee—took off for a Canadian canoe trip that day.

I had always wondered how Helen got Jack to let her go on Canadian canoe trips with former Camp Minocqua campers and counselors during that time. It turns out she made a deal with him: She would go on after-camp Canadian canoe trips, and in return she wouldn't kick him out for his scandalous behavior with his latest girlfriend (by that time he wasn't even trying to keep his affairs a secret). I suspect he had kept her up until the wee hours on the night before the trip, as was his wont when he was displeased with her for whatever reason, and she finally broke—but not in the way one might have expected She rebelled, and began doing the things she had always wanted to do.

Ron must have enjoyed that trip, because a few years later he and his new wife took their honeymoon on another wilderness Canadian canoe trip with Helen, the camp caretaker, and one of Ron's cousins.

The day came when Helen's four older children got together and decided to sit her down and talk with her about why she stayed with Jack. He had been on and off the wagon over the years—more often off than on. The four of us were unanimous in our belief that our two young sisters would be much better off growing up without their father's influence. As I said at the time, "Growing up with him was hell; we don't want Ann and Jennie to go through what we did." When we confronted Helen, she did not disagree, but wondered if a single woman would be able to run a boys' camp by herself. As it happened, Dare and his fiancée, Mary, were about to get married, and were willing to run the camp with Helen if Jack was out of the picture. Everything coincided, and Helen divorced Jack after 31 years of marriage.

Free at Last

So Helen got up the gumption to kick Jack out and found she had a camp to run at the same time she was raising two young girls. She had been pretty much running the camp anyway all those years that Jack was drinking his way through life, and even though he had done his best to convince her she couldn't do anything right without his supervision, she had confidence in her abilities. And Dare was there to help out.

Jack apparently didn't believe what was happening. Even after being kicked out, moving to Chicago, and getting a job selling camping equipment in a department store, he still thought he was going back to Camp Minocqua the following summer. He had been invited to Dare and Mary's wedding in April—not too long after he had moved to Chicago—only on the condition that he behave. He did behave, but when he said to Dare as he was leaving, "I'll see you this summer," Dare's response was "The hell you will."

Of course, Helen didn't legally own the camp until after the divorce was final. And therein lies a tale about the good luck that was to follow her for the rest of her life. When the camp incorporated, Jack got 49 shares and Helen got 49. The other two shares went to their longtime friend and camp caretaker, Don Jesse, as a token of appreciation for his friendship and his dedication to the camp. When negotiations during the divorce failed to produce any kind of agreement on ownership of the camp, Don signed his two shares over to Helen, in spite of pressure from Jack not to do so. So it was actually Don who saved the camp for Helen. He continued as caretaker until the camp closed, using his skills and inventiveness to keep the physical and mechanical parts of the camp going long after many of them should have given out.

Helen's social ease, her optimism, and her lack of fear all served her to good stead when she took over the camp promotional trips by herself. She had done them every winter with Jack, but her role had been more procedural than substantive—organizing the visits, making sure the movie projector worked and that they had brought the right films, following up with letters to prospective camp parents. But she easily stepped right into the promotional role.

Helen hadn't come from money, but she had no trouble hobnobbing with really rich people in Chicago. She was well educated and well read, and could fit in anywhere, socially and intellectually. She was never self-conscious about anything, so she was as comfortable in an upper-class city world as she was in the woods—although her sensible shoes and tweedy skirts or slacks always made her look like she belonged more in the woods than in the city. But then, looking "woodsy" was not a drawback for a camp director.

Helen's attitude toward getting along with the "upper class" was reflected in a story she loved to tell about her husband's sister. Muffy's entire life was spent showing her social circle that she was a master of the requisite graces. Shortly after Jack and Helen were married, while still living in Chicago, Helen was invited to a tea. Muffy was horrified when Helen showed up without a hat, which just wasn't done on the north shore of Chicago in the 1930s. As always, Helen was not the least bit self-conscious or repentant, and her retelling of the story over the years shows her disdain for the idea that she should mold her behavior to other people's norms.

The promotional trips for the camp did create a dilemma for Helen, however: what to do with her two young daughters while she was away. Jack had always spent money the family didn't have, so before the divorce, nannies were hired to come in and care for the house and the children during the promotional trips. When Helen did them by herself, she was trying to watch expenses, so she sometimes took Ann and Jennie with her. They enjoyed the freedom of traveling and the time spent with their mother—Jennie said she always felt blessed because Helen didn't have a "regular job," and could spend time with her daughters. Other times, Helen "farmed out" the girls to various family members while she was traveling. They stayed with Dare and Mary in the Anchor one winter, and spent another winter with me and my family when we had rented a house that had an extra bedroom. Helen even drove the girls to New Brunswick to stay with Ron while he was house-sitting there.

Ron's description of the border crossing into Canada when Helen drove all of them to New Brunswick is hilarious. Ann was in sixth grade, Jennie in third. They were departing from Minocqua right after Christmas, and Helen didn't want to leave her decorated Christmas tree behind, so she put it in the van. She then loaded up Ron, Ann, Jennie, and herself, and took off for the east coast. They picked up a friend in Chicago and a hitchhiker somewhere along the way. After stopping to see me in Massachusetts, they drove across Maine to the New Brunswick border. It was almost midnight on New Year's Eve, and Helen still had the Christmas tree in the van, along with two young girls and three twenty-something men. The border guard started asking the usual questions: Where do you live? Where are you going? What's your purpose? The more answers he got, the more confused and suspicious he became. These are your daughters? You're 54 years old and you have an eight-year-old daughter? You're going to New Brunswick so your son can take care of your daughters there? What are you doing that you can't take care of them yourself? Your son quit his teaching job to take care of them? How can he take care of them if he's not making any money? That one's a hitchhiker? You put your daughters in danger by picking up an unknown hitchhiker?

Thus what was a perfectly ordinary family trip from the Broomell perspective turned into an investigation into a possible kidnapping. They were all interviewed by the head customs officer, each in separate rooms to see if their stories matched. The customs officer even called the principal of the school in New Brunswick where the girls were enrolled, disturbing his New Year's Eve celebration to verify that Ann and Jennie were really scheduled to start school there in January. Eventually, the officials were convinced that everything was perfectly all right, and Ann and Jennie stayed with Ron for three months.

An attractive, vivacious divorcée in her early fifties was bound to attract men, especially since she was by nature so outgoing with everybody. There were older men and younger men, men she got very involved with and men she partied with and abandoned. Unfortunately, Helen was attracting some men who were too much like Jack. Her longtime companion Ed was so domineering that he came very close to being abusive. At one point, he was being particularly nasty to her, and Helen turned to a friend and commented, "It's hard work being a mistress." Although Ed was a good companion for her wilderness adventures, she finally got fed up and left him during an organized group trip to the Canyonlands National Park in Utah. His selfishness had begun to affect the whole group, and Helen finally said, "Enough!" She went back to Wisconsin without him, and that was the end of that.

It certainly wasn't the end of Helen's interest in men, however. Her friend Bev tells a story about driving in Canada on their way to pick up a Camp Minocqua canoe trip. When they had gotten "so far up north that there were still tepees back in the forest," they encountered a backwoods inn in the middle of nowhere, so old-fashioned that it still had separate entrances for men and women. It was warm inside, and there were quite a few people sitting around talking. Helen was fascinated by a "youngish-old man with a ponytail," as Bev described him, "who stood very straight and used his body well." Helen watched him during dinner, speculating on what he did and what he was doing there. After a trip to the powder room, she came back and told Bev that she had met the man on the stairs. Helen proceeded to talk about pursuing him, only half teasingly. Bev thought it was "so cool that a woman her age would be interested in pursuing a guy, for whatever reason."

"HELEN WAS A BABE!"
(Beverly Plummer, friend)

Helen had a knack for befriending people, which is nicely captured in a quote from her artist friend Jim. Speaking of the many friends she had made, he said, "And that's it ... she met people and made friends of them ... simply that." Anybody was welcome in Helen's life, no matter their reasons for being there, who they were, or what they might have done in the past. Her kindness to everybody she met became more apparent after Jack was no longer around to put her down for helping people she didn't know. She had an amazing ability to meet whatever needs anybody had, and she was always able to help people gain confidence in themselves just by listening to them. She never told anybody what to do, even when asked, but her faith in their goodness and their abilities came through in her dealings with family, friends, and even strangers. She might not be able to solve all their problems, but somehow she always had the wisdom to help in some way. Perhaps one of the things Helen always did best was to make other people feel good about themselves.

My son Dan gave a good example of this ability. As a child, he always knew his grandmother was an unusual person. Other kids' grandmothers didn't do flips off diving boards, or stand on their heads on surfboards, or make venison jerky in their kitchen ovens. To him, she was like "a person of mythical proportions." When Dan was older, he did a solo cross-country bicycle trip. This was after Helen's Alaskan adventures, and Dan was telling her about his experiences on his bike trip. Her response was, "You're awesome." Just those two words made him feel "amazingly good," coming from a person who had done everything Helen had.

Dan's older brother Manuel told of childhood memories of a grandmother whose "enthusiasm for everyday life was contagious." He said that even at a fairly young age, he recognized that her kindness stemmed from a total acceptance of other people in a nonjudgmental way. He particularly remembers an interesting conversation he once had with Helen. Manuel has always been a Grateful Dead fan, and he figured that because Helen's children all enjoyed good music and "had that hippy vibe going on at times in their lives," she would understand "the hippy band rock-and-roll mentality." So he started talking about how special the Grateful Dead were, how inspiring their music was, how they had created a counter-culture of kind and friendly people, and how it all reminded him of the accepting, nonjudgmental nature of Helen, her family, and the north woods. After prattling on for a time, Manuel realized that Helen had no idea who the Grateful Dead were, but when she said, "That's nice," it was obvious she really meant it.

Talking about Helen's intrepid spirit, Manuel claimed that "Helen passed on a great deal of adventurousness to me; however, mine pales in comparison to hers. Hers is more serene and balanced ... the difference is in the inner peace that Helen was able to achieve. Her adventures on the Yukon River have always been a source of pride and wonder for me." Manuel says that even now "her spirit still lingers in approval" whenever he thinks about her.

Dare's daughter Lynda recounted the same kind of warm memories of sitting and talking with her grandmother. She used to walk from Dare's house to Helen's house on weekend mornings, and always felt special because of Helen's interest in what she was doing. Helen's "calmness and matter-of-fact way always put things in perspective," Lynda related. "Later in life, I realized that she was like that with everyone. What a wonderful gift she gave us all by just being Helen."

This ability to make other people feel good about themselves resulted in people Helen just happened to meet becoming important parts of her life. From the time Jack left until she got Alzheimer's, if there was an empty bed anywhere around, whoever happened along was welcome to stay. If there were no empty beds, there was always "plenty of room on the floor" (a line from a song Helen's son Ron wrote at about that time). Some people stayed the night, others stayed a week or so, some became permanent fixtures in Helen's life. Her close friend Peggy was one of the latter. The two women had talked with each other before Peggy dropped into Helen's life, but they had never formally met. Peggy was an artist, and Helen had attended all her exhibits, always congratulating her and telling her how much she liked her work. When Peggy met Ron—in his mid thirties, not yet settled down, and staying at the time on Camp Minocqua's little island—she accepted his invitation to stop by Helen's house sometime for a visit. So one day soon after the invitation, there came a knock on Helen's door; she opened it, and immediately recognized Peggy.

Helen reacted the way she always reacted to people: with profuse exclamations of how glad she was to see them, come in, sit down, how are you, tell me all about yourself. Peggy asked after Ron. "Oh, he's on the island. I can take you over." She then took Peggy down to the dock, helped her into a rowboat, and rowed her out to the island, all the while asking questions about Peggy and repeating how wonderful it was that she was there. Peggy had never met anybody like Helen—she didn't even know anybody who could row a boat! She kept thinking, "What kind of woman would interrupt whatever she was doing to row somebody she didn't know to an island? And carry on such a lovely, matter-of-fact conversation while doing it?" Peggy said she was "blown away."

Over the next two years, Peggy stayed in the Screen House for months on end while she was trying to make a

"THE BEST LITTLE PLACE TO SLEEP ON TOMAHAWK LAKE"
(As attested to by the many people who have slept there)

living as an artist. (The Screen House is a rustic two-room cabin right on the shore of the lake, which served as Helen's three-season "guest house" for many years. With the lake shore only a few feet away, and nothing between the bedroom and the outside except screening and a roll-down bamboo curtain, it is a delightful place to sleep.) Peggy was raising two children by herself, and her car wasn't reliable enough to get her to her job painting sets at a local summer theater. Helen gave Peggy and her children a place to sleep and a vehicle to use when Peggy's wouldn't start. Peggy later bought a rustic cabin that had been owned by one of the original Camp Minocqua counselors, thus becoming a year-round neighbor of Helen's and the most permanent of the drop-in friends in Helen's life.

Peggy said she had never met anybody as comfortable, casual, and brave about life as Helen was, and this attitude became a role model for her in many ways. She credits Helen with getting her through her divorce, with teaching her how "to look at things," and with teaching her how to raise her children. Helen later confided to Peggy, however, that she wished she had been a better mother herself. "I regret all those years I put my children through the chaos of my marriage," Helen said. "If I could do it over again, I would do it very, very differently."

Another near-permanent fixture in Helen's life was her handyman Kevin. He was a man of indeterminate years—younger than Helen but older than Ken and Ron—who appeared in Helen's life somehow; nobody in the family is quite sure how. He needed work, and Helen needed a handyman. She had very little money to pay anybody, but she had lots of places for people to sleep. So she traded a place to live for Kevin's odd jobs. For years, he cut and stacked her firewood, shoveled her snow, and kept her house in repair. Even after the camp closed, causing a dramatic reduction in the number of available sleeping spaces, Helen always found a place for Kevin, and he always did whatever work she needed done.

One of Helen's most characteristic traits was her ability to go through life without worrying about anything. A good example of this comes from one of her promotional trips to Chicago, when she stayed with friends who lived on the south side of the city. When returning late at night from evening meetings with prospective camp parents, she often had to park many blocks from her friends' house and walk back alone, through a neighborhood that could be intimidating even during the day, much less late at night, and for a woman alone and carrying a movie projector. When asked if she wasn't afraid, she replied, "You just walk like you belong there, and people leave you alone."

This same lack of worry was evident later in the freedom she allowed her two young daughters (and of course in her own fearlessness on her Alaskan trips). When Ann was about thirteen, she asked if she could go on a bicycle trip to Chicago with two guys. Helen said no, but as a "consolation prize," Ann was allowed to go backpacking alone in the Porcupine Mountains for four days. Mary asked Helen, "What if she's not there when you go to pick her up?" Typically, Helen's reply was, "She'll be there." And of course she was.

A few years later, Ann, still a teenager, hitchhiked from her school in Maine to my house in Massachusetts, sleeping on beaches along the way, and later hitchhiked from New Brunswick to Wisconsin with a Great White Pyrenees dog in tow. No worries.

There are innumerable accounts of Helen's calmness in the face of difficulties. When Ken fell while downhill skiing, the two large gashes on his forehead were bleeding so profusely that a woman fainted when he and Helen walked into the ski chalet, both covered with blood. While everybody else was freaking out, Helen was calmly saying, "Well, maybe we need to do something here. Let's see what we need." She just figured that if Ken had been able to walk down the ski hill all right, he couldn't be hurt too badly, so why worry.

That same calmness was evident during one of Peggy's frequent coffee-and-conversation visits to Helen. It was winter, and Peggy had taken her two preteen children along. She and Helen were sitting snugly inside Helen's house while Peggy's children played outside. Suddenly Peggy's daughter started screaming that her brother had fallen through the ice. Helen and Peggy ran outside, and saw a hole in the ice, fairly far out in the bay, but they couldn't see the boy. Helen finally spotted him climbing up on shore, and she matter-of-factly took him up to the house, put him in a warm bathtub, dried him and warmed him up, gave him a cup of tea, and went back to her conversation with Peggy as if nothing had happened.

There are many other stories in the same vein. Helen never got flustered about anything in her life. She just accepted whatever came at her, so nothing ever threw her for a loop. Her reaction was always, "OK, this is what it is; we'll deal with it from here."

After her divorce, Helen was always ready for a party. Many were spontaneous; old camp people would drop in to say hello, and Helen would call up anybody who was around who might or might not have known them. All of a sudden it was a party. And Helen had an amazing knack for producing an outstanding dinner for a dozen people in half an hour out of nothing but what she could find in her kitchen cupboard.

Because this was the late 1960s and early 1970s, and because most of the people who went to these parties were young, there was a group of "regulars" that Mary described as "Helen's hippies: old Camp Minocqua people drinking and drugging." Helen was never interested in drugs; for her, life was always interesting enough without having to augment it. And over thirty years of living with an alcoholic had cured her of any desire for alcohol. But she loved the sociability of a party, and if it was summer, she loved the skinny dipping that was invariably part of any warm-weather party. My first husband and I were present at one of those parties, where Helen first stood on her head for twenty minutes, and then went skinny dipping. That experience was probably key to my husband deciding that my mother was a bad influence on me. But skinny dipping, and saunas, were just natural to Helen, not awkward or embarrassing in any way.

Although most of the parties during those years were totally spontaneous, there was at least one that was very carefully planned. When her good friend Beverly had an art book published, Helen decided to celebrate with a "literary tea," to be held at Camp Minocqua's Pioneer Camp—a rustic compound of log buildings built by campers over the years, in a remote wooded location on the Tomahawk River. Helen sent out formal invitations, and everybody came in costume. There were magicians, bears, circus performers, a priest, and other creatures not normally found in the north woods. As Bev described it, anybody chancing on the gathering would have thought it strange indeed that the woods were full of such beings as these. Bev herself—who was seldom seen in anything other than blue jeans—wore a prom dress, a huge hat with flowers on it, gloves up to her elbows, an oversize corsage Helen had given her, and long underwear under the dress. The long underwear was not meant to be part of the costume—it was October, and it was cold, and most literary teas are not held in a log cabin in the woods with no electricity and no running water.

Although the party was dubbed a literary tea, no tea

"EVERYTHING WAS OVERDONE AND VERY CLASSY"
(Beverly Plummer, friend, shown at the literary tea in her honor)

was served; it was punch instead. Bev described the punch as a "killer": a mix of various kinds of alcohol and fruit juices, served in a pumpkin with holes cut around the top for inserting straws, and called a "Rumpunchkin." The rustic setting, costumes, formal attire, and goofy people were already making the party funny; the punch made it even funnier. Helen had brought a stack of Bev's books for her to sign for guests, and as the afternoon and evening wore on, Bev admitted that the inscriptions in the books were becoming increasingly ridiculous.

A number of people were found passed out in various places in the morning, so Helen decided that Rumpunchkin was way too dangerous, and never made it again.

Just as Helen's motto for parties was always "the more the merrier," her motto for car trips was "take anybody who wants to go." So on a family trip to northern Ontario to ride the Polar Bear Express to Hudson Bay, she started out with six people in the van: herself, her son Ron (with guitar), her daughter Ann (with flute), her daughter Jennie, and her good friends Bev and John. They stopped to have dinner with some other artist friends who lived about an hour north of Minocqua. Over dinner Helen was describing the planned trip, and her friends' two adolescent children got very excited—wouldn't it be wonderful if they could do something like that? Helen's reaction to that was "Why not come along? There's always room for two more." The parents agreed the children could go, so they packed up, and in the morning there were eight people in the van. Then Helen started picking up hitchhikers. She liked to pick up hitchhikers whenever she was on a road trip, but not any old hitchhikers. She never picked up "ordinary" people; it had to be some-body interesting looking, or somebody with a dog, or a cat, or a child. "That looks like a good one," she'd say, "let's pick him up." By the time they left Wisconsin, they had ten people in the van, making it quite crowded, but Helen didn't notice. Bev claimed they eventually had twelve people in the van, but couldn't remember who the other two were. More hitchhikers?

Even when an event wasn't a party, Helen could turn it into one. Once when she, Ron, and Ann were at a bluegrass concert in the auditorium of a nearby high school, with seats in the very first row, the band started playing a traditional Irish tune. Helen's enthusiasm got the better of her, and she sprang to her feet and started to demonstrate her perfect form with a jig. Ann joined her, and soon they had many other people dancing in the aisles. (Ann and Jennie both inherited Helen's love of dancing. Helen often said that Jennie came out of the womb dancing, and Ann has been dancing her way through life for many years.)

Jennie's impression of her mother during those years was that Helen came alive after Jack was gone—it was like a new person had been born. Helen was free to be herself; she didn't have to try to be what someone else wanted her to be any more, and that gave Jennie encouragement to be free as well.

Helen's own impression of herself during those years was succinct: "You know, it just gets better and better every year."

Jack didn't approve of Helen's lifestyle, and he didn't approve of the way she was raising their daughters. However, he had long since lost whatever influence he may once have had over Helen. Even Ann and Jennie, who had originally enjoyed visiting him in Chicago, grew tired of his harangues against their mother whenever they were there, and refused to go any more. He remarried, and may have had a few happy years—or maybe not—before dying of complications of alcoholism at age 59.

Although Helen's life was clearly improving, there was one thing that wasn't getting better. The cost of running the camp increased dramatically every year, what with real estate taxes, liability insurance, salaries, and the costs of the ever-expanding wilderness canoe tripping program. For a while small increases in tuition made up for it, but there was a point at which tuition increases meant loss of campers. Clearwater Camp solved the problem by switching from one seven-week session to two three-and-a-half-week sessions, but Helen didn't want to do that. In her view, three and a half weeks just wasn't enough time to reap the benefits of the camp experience. She chose instead to sell portions of the land she had inherited from her father. Scattered portions of his early land purchases had not previously been sold, so Helen sold a small piece whenever she needed to balance the camp budget. But there was a limit to that, as she soon started running out of land she was willing to sell.

So in the early 1970s, the decision was made that the only solution was to close Camp Minocqua. As always, Helen did not dwell on the negative side of the situation, instead looking forward to having more time for tripping adventures.

A Tripping Grandmother

ALTHOUGH HELEN HAD BEGUN HER CANOE TRIPS LONG before she closed the camp—even before she divorced Jack—it was only after the camp closed that she was free to do much more than an after-camp Canadian canoe trip once a year. With her children grown and semi-grown, she could now take off more frequently, at any time of the year, by any means of transportation, and go anywhere she wanted to go.

Throughout the 1970s, Helen added hiking and backpacking to her tripping repertoire, going backpacking close to home in the Porcupine Mountains, or on organized trips to places like the Adirondacks. She took Ann along on most of these trips, as well as on many of the canoe trips, but Jennie refused to go, announcing that she much preferred to keep nature on the other side of the window. When asked where she stayed while Helen was off doing wilderness things, Jennie wasn't sure, but she did remember staying home alone a couple of times when she was in middle school.

Jennie enjoyed going along on the road trips, however, which became more frequent, longer, and more spontaneous as time went on. Little planning went into these trips; Helen would decide one evening that she wanted to go halfway across the country to visit a friend, and be off the next day. Once on the road, she went wherever she felt like going, and found a place to camp when she got tired. She was known to invite people she had just met to travel with her, and to pick up hitchhikers along the way. Her invitations were accepted on more than one occasion. I was a little shocked when Helen, Ann, and Jennie arrived in Massachusetts for a visit, accompanied by a hitchhiker and a friend-of-a-friend who Helen had met at a party the evening before she left.

On one of those trips, the place she found to camp when she was tired turned out to be a state park that closed at sundown. Helen arrived about ten o'clock in the evening, with Ann, Jennie, and her friend Bev. They decided that if they found a secluded place to park the van, nobody would bother them, even though they weren't supposed to be there after sundown. At some point after they had all gone to sleep, however, there was a knock on the window of the van. It was the park ranger, who flashed his light around and asked who they were and what they were doing. He seemed horrified that two women and two young girls would be traveling by themselves, much less sleeping in a van in a deserted park. He obviously couldn't let them stay in the park, but neither did he want to send them off to try to find an open motel in the middle of the night. So the ranger asked them to follow him to his house, where they slept peacefully in his driveway, and were sent off the next morning with coffee and homemade bread. There was something about Helen that always brought out the kindness in other people.

Helen's canoe tripping was also becoming more adventurous. The Camp Minocqua Canadian trips had begun with the Minnesota/southern Ontario Boundary Waters, but that was much too populated for Helen's taste. Later trips were out of Armstrong, further north in Ontario, where genuine wilderness was still to be found. Most of these trips were with former Camp Minocqua campers and counselors, and Helen was often the only woman on them. In fact, the wife of a man who wanted to go on one of the trips refused to let her husband go, because Helen was going to be the only woman on the trip.

Helen treated misadventures on canoe trips as she treated all other misadventures—with a shrug of her shoulders. On one of her trips, she and Ann were in an old Camp Minocqua aluminum canoe that got caught on a rock. With the canoe bent around the rock and full of water, there was no way they were going to be able to salvage it. Helen's reaction to losing the canoe, as well as a lot of gear and most of their food, was: "Well, that's just how it is. We'll load up the gear we have and put it in the other canoes." No big deal—nothing ever was for Helen.

After a few years, even the Armstrong wilderness

wasn't enough. Helen's desire for ever more remote wilderness led her to the Churchill River in northern Saskatchewan, which she canoed with her friend Ed. The two of them were dropped off by airplane at the starting point of the trip and scheduled for pickup at the endpoint three weeks later. Before leaving, Helen shocked her pharmacist by presenting him with prescriptions for multiple antibiotics, syringes, and other supplies for medical emergencies. He thought she must be deathly ill, but she quickly reassured him that she was just taking reasonable precautions for the trip she was going on. When I asked her before she left what would happen if she and Ed weren't at the endpoint when they were supposed to be, she just grinned and replied, "I don't worry about things like that."

During that time, Helen added a new kind of trip to her repertoire. Her sister Grace and brother-in-law Bill had been in Florida for the winter, planning to drive back to Wisconsin in the spring. Grace had become ill, however, and couldn't drive, so when spring came, Bill asked Helen if she would be willing to go to Florida and help him drive back. Helen was very happy to help, but had to figure out a way to get to Florida without driving her own car. A bus would take too long, and flying would be too expensive. So she decided to hitchhike.

A Tripping Grandmother

Helen soon discovered that sometimes hitchhiking is easy and sometimes it's impossible. It was impossible on the busy expressways going around Chicago. With multiple lanes of traffic zipping along, nobody was going to stop, even for a harmless-looking grandmother. But somebody did stop—a state trooper. After chastising her for doing something that was not only dangerous, but also illegal, he asked Helen why she was hitchhiking. She explained, in her innocent way, about helping drive her sister and brother-in-law back from Florida. Instead of giving her a ticket, the trooper gave her a ride to the other side of Chicago to be sure she got there safely.

Helen reported after the hitchhiking trip that it was a wonderful way to travel. She had met many interesting people, and the only problem she encountered was one driver who had a very strong southern accent. It wasn't until it was "almost too late" that she realized he was propositioning her.

When somebody later asked Helen if she wasn't worried about being a woman hitchhiking alone, she replied that she was "too old to worry." Her lack of worry may have been a self-fulfilling prophecy, because nothing ever bad ever happened to her on any of her adventures. Her friend Bev later said that nothing bad ever *could* have happened to Helen. "She wasn't expecting evil or harm, so just by the power of who she was, it didn't come to her."

✧✧✧✧✧

In between all of her canoe trips, backpacking trips, and other adventures, Helen decided to organize a Camp Minocqua reunion, to be held in the summer of 1980, seventy-five years after the founding of the camp. It was, not surprisingly, given Helen's talents, very well planned and organized. All the old camp pictures and other memorabilia were displayed, memories flowed freely, old friendships were revived, and a good time was had by all.

For Helen and her six children, the reunion had a delightful side effect. The six siblings were spread out all

FINALLY!
(The first time Helen's six children were all in the same place at the same time)

A Tripping Grandmother

over the country, and although they had been in contact with each other on a fairly regular basis, they had never, in the eighteen years there had been six of them, been in the same place at the same time. It was a momentous occasion, and Helen basked in the pleasure of it.

A couple of years after her Churchill River trip, Helen did a 250-mile river trip by herself, including paddling a 20-pound solo canoe in New Brunswick and on the Allagash River in Maine. She visited me in Massachusetts on her way home from that trip, and took her solo canoe out in the Merrimack River. After all the whitewater canoeing she had done, she assumed that a tidewater river would be a snap. It was, at first. But suddenly she was caught in very strong crosscurrents created by the mix of downriver current, upriver tide, and a narrowing of the river where a bridge crossed it. Her canoeing experience and her determination got her out of what could have been a deadly situation for somebody else. My son Dan later described how watching her battling the rushing waters in that very small, very tippy canoe contributed to his lifelong image of Helen as an almost mythical being.

I also thought she was a somewhat mythical being when I once commented to her, "I don't know how you do all that; I couldn't do it." My mother gave me a sly smile and replied, "Well, I couldn't do it at your age, either, my dear."

But none of this was enough. The ultimate wilderness canoeing experience was Alaska, and Helen hatched a scheme that only she could have come up with. She would paddle down the Yukon River in Alaska, and she would do it by herself!

Unlike her totally spontaneous road trips, Helen's first trip to Alaska was very carefully planned. Couldn't find instant wild rice? She'd make it herself. Didn't like the quality of the beef jerky she found in the stores? She'd make it herself. Couldn't find a tent that met her needs? She'd make it herself. Didn't have a sturdy canoe that was short enough for one person? She'd make it herself. Well, not quite. She had a 17-foot aluminum canoe left from the camp, but it was too long to paddle by herself in a swift river current. So she took the canoe to a local jack-of-all-trades and asked him to cut two feet out of the middle and rivet it back together. He didn't want to do it, saying he couldn't guarantee the rivets would be watertight. She persuaded him to try anyway—she was sure it would be fine. A trial run on Tomahawk Lake proved her right.

But would she be physically able to handle whatever she might encounter while she was alone on the Yukon River? Helen felt she needed to "test her limits," so she

A Tripping Grandmother

signed up for an Outward Bound wilderness course. She had no problems whatsoever carrying a pack, climbing up and rappelling down cliffs, mastering the ropes course, or doing an overnight solo in the woods. But she couldn't run as far as she was supposed to. No problem—you can't run very far on a river anyway.

One of Helen's favorite anecdotes from that period is about guns. A friend asked her if she was taking a gun with her to Alaska, for protection from the bears. "Oh no," replied Helen, "I'd be more afraid of the gun than I would be of the bears."

Another good story about the preparations for her first trip to Alaska tells about how Helen managed to get a senior citizens' pass for the Alaska Ferry system. Having a pass allowed the holder to ride free on any state-run ferry during off seasons. The minimum age to get a pass, however, was 65, and Helen was only 64 that summer. Her solution was simple: She altered her driver's license by removing the first digit from the numeral 12, thus changing her birth month from December to February, so she appeared to be ten months older than she really was. Nobody ever noticed that her license then said she had been born on the 31st of February.

Helen ended up doing two separate Yukon River canoe trips. The first started at Dawson City in Canada's

Yukon Territory and went to the pipeline bridge over the Yukon River north of Fairbanks. The second, two years later, began at the pipeline bridge and finished at St. Mary's, about 100 miles from the Bering Sea. Those trips are described in her two books, *Solo on the Yukon* and *Solo on the Yukon Again;* the books also include narrations of Helen's Alaskan hitchhiking and backpacking adventures, historical and geographic information about the places she visited, and descriptions of the many unique friends she made.

Two aspects of Helen's Alaskan trips tell a lot about who she was: the fact that a 64-year-old grandmother would even think about paddling down the Yukon River by herself, and the ease with which she met and was befriended by such a large number of extraordinary people during her travels. That combination of love of solitude and love of people was one of the things that made Helen unique.

Helen was welcomed and feted in every native village she stopped in along the river. The innate native respect for the elderly, combined with Helen's openness, her interest in other people, and her love of the wilderness, made her immediately welcome every place she went. If she had already set up camp before she went into a village, the people would insist she stay another night so they could show her their hospitality. She ended up spending three extra nights in one town along the river to avoid arguments about who she would stay with.

A Tripping Grandmother

The friends Helen met and made along the way were extraordinary, and with them she was able to experience Alaska in ways she never could have by herself. All of them remained friends for the rest of her life: she visited them on every later trip she made to Alaska, and corresponded with them frequently until her memory failed.

The first of Helen's many Alaskan friends was Ed, who drove her there on her first trip. Ed had caught "Alaska fever" years before, and went there every summer to work as a carpenter. The story of how Helen hooked up with Ed is typical of her. With a limited budget and a 15-foot canoe, flying was out of the question. Driving would entail complications about what to do with her car while she was on the river, and how to get the car to her takeout spot. In her book she says only that a "friend of a friend came to the rescue." She doesn't mention that he was a "friend of a friend" only coincidentally—she had actually met him by putting a notice on the Ride Board at the University of Wisconsin in Madison: "Old woman with canoe needs ride to Alaska." The "friend" of whom Ed was a friend was someone Helen barely knew then, but who would later become her son-in-law.

Then there were Celia and Ginny, a pair of women who were true characters. Both had ferried fighter planes during World War II; after the war they founded a rustic resort outside McKinley Park and ran it for 25 years.

When they sold it, they retired to their wilderness cabin and became environmental activists.

There were also Mary and John, a young couple whose summer cabin could only be reached by a mile and a half of "very obscure trail," and whose winter cabin was even more inaccessible. They worked periodically, but only enough so they could afford to pursue their passion: breeding, keeping, and running sled dogs. Both had run the Iditarod, and Mary was the only person who had ever run it to the end and then turned right around and run it back—she wanted to go back and thank all the people along the way for the hospitality they had provided her.

Finally there were Jan and Ed, a couple who picked Helen up while she was hitchhiking. Their remote cabin made Mary and John's seem almost suburban. It was accessible only by driving fifteen miles out from town on a dirt road, then walking a mud road, then hiking a winding path down the edge of a canyon, and then scampering down a steep cliff to a beautiful grassy slope above a bay.

At the end of her first Alaskan canoe trip, Helen had paddled halfway down the Yukon River. She left her canoe at a gas station near the pipeline bridge over the Yukon, where the owner had agreed to try to sell it for her and send her the money. By the time she got back

A Tripping Grandmother

to Wisconsin in mid-November—after staying in Alaska longer than planned so she could go dogsledding with her friend Mary—she had changed her mind about selling the canoe. In reality, Helen may have decided to return to Alaska long before she got home, but the story she always told was that she decided on her way back. EIther way, as soon as she got home, she immediately called the gas station owner to ask him if he would store her canoe for her until she returned—she was going to go back and paddle down the rest of the Yukon!

So a year and a half later, Helen was off to Alaska again. Her brother-in-law restored antique cars and was going to see a collector in Edmonton, Alberta. He was happy take her along, and to continue on and drop her at the Alaska Ferry terminal in Prince Rupert, British Columbia. After the ferry trip and an easy hitch to Anchorage, she ended up getting a ride to Homer with Ed, the same "friend of a friend" who had driven her to Alaska on her first trip. He was in the same van, with the same daughter, and the same daughter's friend. As if that weren't luck enough, a few days later the four of them found themselves paddling the clear, cold lakes of a wilderness state park that had no access except by boat or plane. In her words, "With the white-capped peaks reflected in it, each lake was a perfect gem." Good luck seemed to follow Helen around everywhere she went.

She spent more time being "touristy" on her second trip than on the first. What she enjoyed most was "just walking around, soaking in the atmosphere, and talking to the people." But after a few weeks of that, she was ready to get back on the river. She hitched a ride to the pipeline bridge north of Fairbanks and set off, with no plans for specific places to stop or specific times to be anywhere. "No schedules, no plans, seems to work for me," she wrote in her second book.

Helen seemed to revel in whatever weather was thrown at her during her Alaskan trips. She described a week of river rafting in cold rain, wind, and even snow as "invigorating." On one of her ferry trips, she had a 12-hour layover before the returning ferry stopped to take passengers back. She was never one to sit around for twelve hours when there were places to explore, so she gathered a group of her fellow passengers and went on a hike. It didn't matter that it was raining, or that none of them had brought extra clothing to change into. After the hike, they managed to find a laundromat so they could dry their wet clothes, but as she said in *Solo on the Yukon Again,* "The dilemma involved in getting out of wet clothes, drying them and then dressing again in a public place was something to laugh at." Many of her readers must have wished she had provided more details on just how that was done.

The only time Helen admitted to being concerned

A Tripping Grandmother

about weather was at the end of her second Yukon trip. She may have been spontaneous and carefree, but she was not foolhardy. As she got closer to the Bering Sea, the weather deteriorated. After she had paddled for several days in high winds and heavy rains, gotten marooned on a sandbar, and spent an extra day stuck at a "barely adequate" campsite, she concluded that the river was "starting to tell me to think about leaving it." She didn't want to end her trip where she was, however, because she had tickets for an airplane tour starting at St. Mary's, about 100 miles downriver. As usual, her good luck came to her aid. She shared lunch one day with an Eskimo family along the river, and when she asked if they knew of anybody who might be willing to give her a boat ride down the last 100 miles of the river in exchange for her canoe, they took her up on the deal. She got what she needed, with a minimum of fuss, even if she had to give up her canoe to do it. One might think Helen would have wanted to preserve that canoe as a memento of her adventures, but, practical as always, she simply said, "I couldn't have gotten it back to Wisconsin anyway."

Helen came back from both Alaskan canoe trips with some fabulous stories. One of her favorites had to do with a bear. She hadn't taken a watch to Alaska with her, so while she was on the river, she simply stopped each day when she was beginning to tire and looked for an island in the river where she could camp without worrying about bears getting into her food. One day she couldn't find an island to camp on when she was ready to stop, so when she spotted a large tree blown down over the bank of the river, she paddled over, tied her canoe to a branch of the tree, lay down in the bottom of the canoe, and went to sleep. Some time later—Helen had no idea how much time had passed, and the June midnight sun was no help—she awoke to a strong shaking of the canoe. When she opened her eyes, the cause of the shaking was obvious: A large brown bear was sitting on the tree trunk, shaking the branch her canoe was tied to. Unafraid, but nonetheless deeming it prudent to encourage the bear to leave, she banged as hard as she could on the sides of her aluminum canoe. Nothing happened. More banging. The bear kept right on shaking the branch.

Well, if the bear wasn't going to leave, Helen would have to be the one to do so. Very slowly, and very carefully—but seemingly without a tinge of fear—she got out a knife, crawled to the front of the canoe, and cut the rope. As the canoe began floating slowly downriver, the bear looked a little puzzled, and then began loping along the bank, watching her. Helen never could figure out if it was looking for a meal or just some companionship.

Another of her favorite stories had to do with repaying the hospitality she was shown all over Alaska, which she usually did by helping with whatever chores needed doing. So one day she found herself helping out in a fish camp along the Yukon. The villagers were honored to have her working alongside them, and at dinner that night they showed their gratitude and respect by serving her the greatest delicacy they had: fish eyes. She reports in her book that she did not eat them, but the story changed over time—as all good stories do—and later versions related that although she was not at all thrilled about eating them, she had to do so to avoid insulting her hosts.

After her Alaskan canoe trips, Helen became a minor celebrity in Minocqua—and indeed throughout the whole state. Articles from both trips had been published in the local newspaper; Helen enjoyed calling herself the "first foreign correspondent for *The Lakeland Times*," since the first few articles were written while she was still in Canada. She was in great demand as a speaker to local groups. The articles were later published as books, and she began to get invitations from all over the state to be interviewed, speak, or appear on TV.

Even as she was basking in all the attention she was getting from her books and her speaking engagements, however, Helen remained a very private person. During a discussion with her friend Peggy about people's reactions to her two books, Peggy mentioned that she

HELEN'S FAVORITE PICTURE OF HERSELF
(In Alaska, of course)

always wished the books had included more on how Helen felt about all the things she experienced. Helen looked at her and said, "Why? That's nobody's business." Helen's feelings were always private, not to be shared with anybody except her closest friends.

After the two Yukon River trips, Helen returned to Alaska every other year for the next eight years. She did a coastal kayak trip, backpacked in the Brooks Range, went dog sledding, took the ferry to Kodiak Island, hitchhiked a lot, and spent time with her friends. Since she didn't have to take a canoe along, she drove to Alaska on several of those trips. She still enjoyed road trips, and had fixed herself up with a cute little pickup with a cap, custom-sewn turquoise curtains to fit the windows of the cap (she made them herself, of course), and a foam pad in the bed of the truck. A place to stretch out and a camp stove were all she needed for her "mini motor home." She didn't even really need the foam pad—she was perfectly content when visiting friends or family to sleep on a bare floor with a blanket thrown over her and her clothes for a pillow.

One of the summers Helen didn't go to Alaska, she went on a very memorable road trip. She had been friends for some time with Vernon Kruger, a canoe enthusiast who still, posthumously, holds the world's record for most miles ever paddled by one person. Back then, he had entered the Mississippi River Challenge to try to break the record for the shortest time paddling the full length of the Mississippi River. This 62-year-old man, with his 33-year-old female canoeing partner, was trying to break a record set by two men in their thirties, and Helen was part of his support team. For 23 days and 10 hours, starting in Minnesota and ending at the Gulf of Mexico, Helen drove her pickup from each pre-arranged stopping point to the next, delivering food, first aid, and support to her friends. With her help—and that of many other people—they broke the record, which then held for another five years.

Between trips to Alaska, Helen loved staying at Pioneer Camp—first for a few days at a time, then a week, and finally months at a time. At first she didn't even have a telephone, but Dare got tired of having to drive the two-rut road all the way into Pioneer to deliver messages to her. She also got snowed in at one point, and Dare had to call the police to go in and make sure she was all right. So she reluctantly had a telephone installed.

Helen lived every day of her life in her own way—at least after her divorce—but it is always the special occasions that create some of the most vivid memories. Her daughter Ann's wedding was one special occasion that demonstrated how Helen continued having fun and just being herself into her later years. Ann married Jack (the man who was the friend of Ed, who had driven Helen to Alaska the first time she went) on the Camp Minocqua point on a beautiful June day in one of Helen's "off years" for going to Alaska. It was an amazing wedding; even though Helen didn't have a lot to do with the planning of it, it was her kind of party—casual, friendly, with lots of good music, good cheer, and good food (the reception was potluck). The people who gathered for the occasion included everybody from relatives in conventional wedding attire, to full-leather-clad biker friends, and more than a few seniors in wheelchairs from the nursing home where Ann worked. Add to that a wedding party that looked like a group of 1960s flower children, and you have one of the most eclectic gatherings of people ever seen on the point. I always wished I had written a wedding announcement for the local paper: "The barefoot bride was charming in a yellow sundress with flowers in her hair. The groom was elegant in sandals, white trousers, purple shirt, and yellow headband. The mother of the bride wore a bedspread." In reality, it was a very becoming caftan, but it had begun life as an Indian madras bedspread.

At another wedding during those years, Helen also made an impression on everybody, as usual. The celebration of my second marriage took place on New Year's Eve (coincidentally, Helen's birthday), at the remote Cardigan Ski Lodge in New Hampshire. Helen had been looking forward to joining the backcountry skiing on the day before the wedding, as she was an accomplished cross-country skier. When we set out, everything was fine as long as we were going uphill. But then we came to a point where the narrow trail went down a steep hill and made a sharp turn at the bottom to cross a frozen stream. All of a sudden, I realized that Helen's cross-country skiing experience on the relatively flat trails of northern Wisconsin was nothing like this. I stopped at the top of the hill, turned around, and said to my 68-year-old mother, "You do know how to pole drag, don't you?" Helen's reply: "What's that?" I gave her a short explanation and demonstration, told her to watch me as I went down, and continued very slowly to the bottom of the hill, using my ski poles as a brake. When I turned around to coach Helen down the hill, she was already halfway down, rolling head over heels behind me. Typically, she just got up, brushed the snow off, and said, "It was easier that way."

At my wedding ceremony the next day, Helen was resplendent in Alaskan mukluks, blue jeans, and her favorite blue and turquoise vest (all very appropriate for the occasion, since the bride and groom were attired in Irish fisherman knit sweaters and old blue jeans with red bandanas in our back pockets). Helen began the ceremony by invoking the sprits of Mount Cardigan, but then forgot to disinvoke them before she left to go back to

Invoking the spirits of Mount Cardigan
(At Sue's second wedding)

Wisconsin. My new husband and I were snowed in on our honeymoon with eighty high school students who had rented the lodge for the weekend after our wedding.

A third wedding showed how important Helen's friends were to her. Her artist friend Jim related that he and his later-to-be-wife Sandy had "first basked in that smile and welcoming gaze, not to mention the strong hug" several years before they were married. Jim shared Helen's love of wilderness canoeing, and shortly after they met, they spent a weekend paddling down the Tomahawk River. "Needless to say, when we said our goodbyes we knew we had to come back," and come back they did. When Jim found himself in need of a place to stay while Sandy went to Europe with a friend, he showed up on Helen's doorstep and asked if he could rent The Pines, a small cabin next to her house. "Well, of course," she replied. (That response was so common with Helen that it became part of the inscription on her memorial rock after she died.) But she was about to leave for an Outward Bound course, and didn't have time to talk about the details. "Oh, we'll talk about rent when I get back," she commented over her shoulder as she walked out the door. Jim responded with, "Great, I guess all I need is the key." And of course, in Jim's words, "There was no key because there were no locks. A metaphor."

Jim and Sandy stayed on in The Pines. Five years later, they decided to get married in August, but Helen

A Tripping Grandmother

had already planned her third trip to Alaska. She was able to change her plans so she could be back in time for the wedding, however, and when the day came, she appeared with a fresh Alaskan salmon. Until the day before the wedding, she had been helping Alaskan friends with their salmon wheel in exchange for room and board and "the pick of the catch." On the same day the salmon was caught, as Jim told it, Helen "hitched a motorized ride down the river to a float plane and some ice, flew to Anchorage and packed the salmon in dry ice, flew home, and prepared the salmon deliciously to be served at our wedding reception."

The reception had been moved indoors, as Jim related, "due to persistent rain on the Camp Minocqua point, and then as the rain lifted we moved everything out to the point (including the dwindling salmon). But, as they say, rain on your wedding day is good luck, and the rain did return, often, with the added show of a double rainbow over the lake and the rainbow of friends, everyone warmed by the ever-welcoming air that surrounded Helen."

As Helen moved from her fifties through her sixties and into her seventies, she remained a very attractive woman. She was perhaps a little thicker around the waist, and the increasing wrinkles on her face gave her a more rugged, outdoorsy look, but she exuded vitality and love of life, which more than made up for any effects of age.

Helen loved her house on the shore of Tomahawk Lake, and her rustic log cabin in the woods of Pioneer Camp, but in Alaska she found kindred spirits and a sense of adventure that fulfilled her; she was truly happy during the years of her Alaskan adventures. In between trips to Alaska, she stayed busy giving talks about them and planning the next one. She was also very involved in collecting artifacts to help launch a historical museum in Minocqua, and was instrumental in getting a building constructed for the museum. When the Minocqua Museum opened, she became its first curator, and continued in that capacity for many years. She had family nearby—her son Dare and his wife Mary lived half a mile up the road, and her brother-in-law Bill, with whom she loved to play Scrabble, was just across the bay. (At one point during those years, her brother-in-law—widower of Helen's older sister Grace—proposed to her. She was very fond of Bill, but would never again give up her independence.)

Helen always planned to paddle down the whole Yukon River a second time, in one summer, when she was eighty, and then retire to her log cabin at Pioneer. Life was good.

But as life has a way of doing, just when everything seemed to be going so well, disaster struck. One evening when she was at Bill's house playing Scrabble, the phone rang. It was a neighbor, with the report that Helen's house appeared to be on fire. She looked out across the bay, and saw the house engulfed in flames. Her first concern was for the historical items that had been entrusted to her care while the Minocqua Museum was being built. She paid scant attention to the fact that all her own possessions, including a wonderful collection of art—her own creations and things given to her by her many artist friends—were going up in smoke and flames. True to her nature, she later commented, "Well, I've been meaning to simplify my life, but not quite this much." When friends extended their sympathy, she often responded, "I didn't know what I was going to do with all my things anyway." The only things that caused her real regret were the loss of the museum items, and the loss of the beautiful handmade mahogany canoe that had been a gift to her father from an early Camp Minocqua family, and had been hanging in her living room.

Helen had always attributed her "no-worry" attitude to her father. "If the main building at Camp Minocqua had ever burned down," she would say, "he would have just surveyed the situation and said, 'All right—let's start rebuilding.'" Helen did exactly that. At the time Camp Minocqua closed, she had moved the camp cook's cabin to a spot on the hill beside her house, remodeled it into a cozy little rental cabin, and named it the Pines. Now she added on to it—a full-sized kitchen, a larger bathroom, and a laundry room—and winterized it better. It was the perfect little house for an independent, single woman.

Old Age

As she moved into her seventies, Helen remained as active as ever. There were every-other-year trips back to Alaska to visit friends and do more hitchhiking and backpacking; her work at the local historical museum, which she had helped found and was now curator of; interviews and speaking engagements about her Alaskan adventures; extensive correspondence with her large circle of friends—not to mention that she was still building stone walls to keep the land under her house from washing onto the road. But she began forgetting things. At first it didn't worry anybody—everybody gets more forgetful in old age. I didn't give it a second thought when I got a thank-you note from her for a gift I hadn't given her. As the memory problems got more serious, Helen worked harder to cover them up, and when she remembered something, she celebrated it. One Christmas, she sent me a down pillow accompanied by a note saying "I didn't forget!" My memory had always been very good, but I had no idea what it was my mother hadn't forgotten.

All of Helen's children had begun to notice similar signs of forgetfulness. But the siblings were spread out from the Caribbean to the East Coast to the Midwest to Hawai'i, and frequent communication had never been deemed necessary in the Broomell family. So none of us knew how serious the problem was.

Helen's close friend Peggy may have been the first to realize that this was more than normal old-age forgetfulness. Peggy would often visit Helen in the afternoon, walking the short trail through the woods from her house to Helen's, where Helen would be waiting with coffee on. One day when Peggy arrived, the living room was a mess, the table was covered with multiple place settings and serving dishes with food in them, and Helen was very angry with Peggy. She ranted on and on about Peggy leaving her with all these children—it was fine to ask her to take care of them every once in a while, but not to leave them all afternoon. Helen complained that the children were very disobedient, and refused to eat their food. Eventually Peggy got Helen calmed down and helped her clean up. Soon Helen had forgotten all about it. Peggy called Helen's oldest son Dare, and Dare scheduled an appointment with a neurologist.

Helen's reaction to all the physical and mental testing during her first visit to the neurologist was typical of her attitude toward life. Toward the end of a long day of answering questions, comparing shapes, doing puzzles, and other such tasks, she was given a blank piece of paper and asked to write a sentence. At this point, most patients are tired of the whole procedure and start complaining: "Aren't we done yet? When can I go home?" Helen wrote: "This is getting to be fun."

Of course, there is nothing fun about Alzheimer's, but that's what the diagnosis was. Many people in her situation react with denial, but Helen acted as if somebody had taken a huge burden off her shoulders. It wasn't her fault that she forgot so many things! She went around gleefully telling people, "You know that disease—the one with the Z? Well, I've got it." It was almost as if she were glad to have been diagnosed with Alzheimer's—as if she had been given permission to not worry about her forgetfulness, and could now stop trying to fight it.

At the same time that Helen seemed glad about the diagnosis, however, she also resisted it. She read a lot about Alzheimer's after she was diagnosed, but insisted that what she was reading wouldn't happen to her. And she got upset about an article in the historical museum newsletter that mentioned her Alzheimer's. She didn't want anybody feeling sorry for her, and she certainly didn't want people to think she was useless. "What do they think this thing is that I've got?" she asked. "Something that they might as well take me out and shoot me?"

The summer after Helen's diagnosis, I spent eight weeks with her in Minocqua, arriving in early July without any idea what to expect. I had heard from Dare and Mary about hallucinations, forgetting what day it was, and obsessions with kids who were supposed to be coming but hadn't yet arrived. I was afraid my mother might not recognize me when I arrived, or might have forgotten I was coming.

But Helen hadn't forgotten; she knew immediately who I was. She had laundered the Screen House bedding and gone to the grocery store for food. But the bedding was still in the dryer, and the food was sitting in two plastic grocery bags in the middle of the living room floor. I had no idea how long it had been there, so as I started down to the Screen House to unpack and get settled in, I reminded her to put the food away.

When I returned, Helen was rummaging through the refrigerator, complaining that she couldn't find the egg rolls she had bought that morning. The grocery bags were still in the middle of the living room floor. Putting the food away, I wondered what we were going to eat for dinner that night. Along with the egg rolls, Helen had bought blueberries, strawberries, crab spread, a box of fancy crackers, and a strawberry coffee cake. No real food, though.

So began a bittersweet summer full of laughter and tears. The hallucinations increased; Helen often saw "little people" who wouldn't go away when she told them to. She even called family or friends—and on one occasion the police—to come and get them out of her house. She constantly set an extra place at the table for the "person" who was sitting on the sofa, or standing by the door, or was coming any minute, or had just left but would be right back. She worried about where the people were who were supposed to be there but weren't, and about having enough food for "the rest of the people."

Helen spent a lot of time that summer sorting through papers, but then never doing anything with them. She would look through a bunch of papers, sort them into piles, clip them together, and then leave them on the desk. She tried to help me sort old Camp Minocqua pictures for a camp reunion later in the summer, but she couldn't do it. When she started cutting pictures out of albums, and even cutting pictures in half—claiming they were duplicates—I finally had to hide the pictures from her.

Helen also lost the ability to recognize common objects: She thought the end of a white boat sticking out from behind a boathouse was a washing machine; a dead tree limb with dried leaves on it was a group of little people dressed in Halloween costumes; a big red flashlight was a fire engine.

Another thing that stands out from that summer was Helen's continuing relationship with campers—except that now the campers existed only in her mind. She saw them everywhere: in the woods, outside her windows, on her sofa, or just standing in a room with her. And they were always disobedient campers, who

"WHAT DO YOU SAY WHEN YOUR
MOTHER DOESN'T RECOGNIZE YOU?"
(Sue, during Helen's last summer at home)

never did what she told them to do. These experiences seemed to upset her more than anything else about her disease. I couldn't help but wonder if Helen had worried about disobedient campers, or about not having enough food for everybody, all through the years she was part of Camp Minocqua. If she did, she never let it show.

The hardest thing for me was when my mother stopped recognizing me. It started on my birthday, when Helen—who had always been shorter than I was, and was getting even shorter in her advancing years—asked me to retrieve a ceramic plate from the top shelf in the kitchen. "I'm going to give it to Sue," she explained politely. "Today's her birthday." When I protested that she shouldn't tell me about it if it was a birthday present, her reply was, "Why, are you Sue?"

What does a daughter do in that kind of situation? If my mother hadn't asked, I wouldn't have corrected her. But she did ask, and I couldn't say, "No, I'm not Sue." So I nodded, feeling like I was just another of the many people who had dropped in and out of my mother's life over the years: starving artists, recovering addicts, hippie friends, transient or long-term lovers. However, I needn't have worried about reminding Helen how forgetful she was getting—she immediately forgot she had asked the question.

All through that summer, Helen still believed she would be able to fulfill her dream of paddling down the whole Yukon River in one season when she was eighty years old, and then retiring to her log cabin at Pioneer (still with no electricity or running water). To test whether another Yukon River trip would be even remotely feasible, Peggy and some friends of hers planned a short overnight canoe trip down the Tomahawk River. Helen did very well the first day, easily paddling the short distance to Pioneer from the bridge where the trip started. That evening, as we cooked over a camp fire and then sat around it talking "girl talk," Helen was quite lucid and animated. But on the second day of the trip, she became paranoid when she saw "people" sitting on the branches of a log that had fallen over the river. Helen had never shown fear of anything before in her life, but she was afraid of those "people," and—unbelievably—said she didn't want to be in the canoe. The paranoia and fear with which she reacted to the hallucination showed that anything like another Yukon River trip was out of the question. In the end, it didn't matter. By the time she turned eighty, she had totally forgotten what she had planned to do.

It may have been Helen's acceptance of her disease and her unwillingness to fight it that hastened its progress. Or perhaps the disease had been much more advanced than anybody knew before it was diagnosed, and she had done a superb job of covering it up for more years than we had realized. For whatever reason, the progression from diagnosis to death was swift. Along the way there were many poignant moments.

It soon became apparent that Helen wasn't going to be able to live alone after I returned to Massachusetts, even with a part-time caregiver. My youngest son, Dan, was footloose at the time, and eager to spend more time with his grandmother while he could. So we arranged for him to come and stay with her. I had to leave before Dan could get to Minocqua from Hawai'i, however, and the caregiver was not working out. The only practical solution was to move Helen into an assisted living facility.

Although she was already settled in assisted living by the time Dan got to Minocqua, he and his aunt Ann thought Helen should have one last fling before descending into the darkness of advanced Alzheimer's. Ann was returning to Fort Myers Beach, Florida, where she and her husband were refurbishing a sailing yacht that was to become their home, business, and playground. She decided it would be a good thing to take Helen along for a visit. The staff at the assisted living facility did not approve of a resident with Alzheimer's going off to Florida with two carefree thirty-somethings—even though one of them was a registered nurse. So, in the words of the other care-free thirty-something, they "absconded with her." (Dan and Ann were only six years apart in age and had both inherited a good bit of Helen's attitude toward life.)

They say people's true personalities emerge as Alzheimer's disease progresses. Worriers worry more. Ornery people get more ornery. Helen got more social, more carefree, more independent, and more uninhibited. Although nothing eventful happened in Florida for most of the visit, the last night they were there certainly made up for that. Ann's husband Jack—another carefree soul—decided to take Helen out to dinner. Dan described the scene in the restaurant: Helen was sitting at the head of the table: in Dan's words, the "elegant, esteemed, honored matriarch surrounded by three rowdy companions." Jack always looked a bit like a pirate captain, and that look was enhanced by a bandana tied around his head with the ends hanging down one side of his face. A "gnarly biker" friend of Jack's was with them. Dan, long and lean with a shaved head, looked like a Buddhist monk, but was perfectly capable of being rowdy. And Helen, Alzheimer's or no, could always join in the spirit of a good party. Apparently they were on the verge of being asked to leave the restaurant when they decided on their own that it was time to go.

With every intention of going straight home, the group somehow ended up in a strip joint. All of them quickly got into the spirit of the place, and Helen began floating from group to group, introducing herself and making friends with everybody there. She soon decided it would be fun to dance with those pretty girls up on the stage, and it was all Dan and Jack could do to keep her from joining the strippers.

The plane trip back to Wisconsin the next day was downright boring compared with the previous evening. But Helen didn't do boring, not even—or especially—while Alzheimer's was taking its toll on her mind. As the plane was taxiing down the runway after landing in Mosinee, she stood up and thanked all the other passengers for coming, as if she had just given one of her talks about Alaska.

As a resident of an assisted living facility, Helen was not the kind who was happy to sit quietly all day watching television, and she soon became known among staff and fellow residents alike for her antics. One day she took everything out of another resident's dresser, laid it all out on a table, and put price tags on it for a yard sale. Often when fellow residents gathered in front of the TV set, Helen would stand up in front of them and begin to talk about her Alaskan adventures. She became very confused when the others politely—or not so politely—asked her to sit down and be quiet so they could watch the show.

Helen's most notorious escapade came when she had apparently been hallucinating that the other residents of the facility were her camp staff members. She was standing in the middle of the living room, delegating responsibilities and trying to make sure people did what they were supposed to: "You get the bus," she said, pointing to one of the residents. "You handle the lunches," "You take care of the games." Nobody was paying any attention to her, of course, and she was getting frustrated with these people. So she put on her backpack and headed out the door, muttering about finding a different camp because she had had it with this one. She made it quite a way down the road before somebody caught up with her and took her back.

Through all of this, Helen maintained her vivacity. With a constant smile on her face, her twinkling eyes peering out from behind large glasses, and her short curly hair—only now becoming speckled with grey—making her look somewhat like the mischievous little girl she had once been, she often seemed like an elderly imp trying to get all the fun she could out of whatever life remained to her.

Later, however, in the Alzheimer's unit of a nursing home, there was little of Helen left. When a visitor first greeted her, there may have been a brief flicker of recognition, but it faded immediately. There were still a few humorous moments, however. While Dare and Mary were visiting one day, she raised her arm trying to get the attention of another resident sitting across the room, and then forgot that her arm was up in the air. "What are you doing?" Dare asked. "Charge!" was her reply.

Old Age

Helen had been a member of the Hemlock Society for many years before she forgot what it was to be a member of anything. She had often said, only semi-jokingly, that if she were ever confined to a wheelchair, her children should push her and the wheelchair over a cliff. But of course, by the time the quality of her life was such that she wouldn't have wanted to live it any more, she had forgotten she wouldn't want to be alive at that point. Her children agreed that what she would have wanted most was to be set adrift to end her days floating down the Yukon River. They equally agreed that it would be impossible to do any such thing.

The end came fast—not recognizing anybody, not able to feed herself, or talk. When Helen could no longer swallow, she was hospitalized. The family agreed that no mechanical means should be used to keep her alive, and the doctor said it would just be a "few days."

Ten days later, she was still hanging in there. Peggy was visiting her one day and noticed that Helen was obviously feeling pain. After three requests to a nurse for pain medication, the answer finally came back: No medication; they didn't want Helen to become addicted. Fed up with that nonsense, Peggy crushed up some aspirin, dissolved it in water, and dribbled it into Helen's mouth. With that, Helen's eyes flew open, she looked steadily at Peggy, and then she laughed and laughed and laughed. Peggy called that their "last monkey wrench together." Helen died the next day.

That was not the end, however. The following summer, Helen's family and friends gathered from near and far on the former Camp Minocqua point to celebrate her life. Her eternal optimism imbued the festivities—when it rained, there were comments that Helen had sent the rain so people would have to get closer together as they crowded under the tent to stay dry. The rainbow after the rain was, of course, a manifestation of Helen. When an eagle appeared in one of the tall Norway pines, everybody murmured that Helen had sent it. We reminisced about what a giving person she was, laughed at stories of some of the crazy things she did, thrilled when her son Ron sang "The Cry of the Wild Goose" in her memory, and cried when Peggy talked about how Helen had taught her how to live and taught her how to die.

Old Age

"SHE TAUGHT ME HOW TO DIE."
(Peggy Grinvalsky, friend)

"HELEN SENT THE EAGLE."
(Guests at Helen's memorial celebration)

To My Yukon Loon Mom

You are what legends live to dream,
You're why a singer sings a song.
Your dance is perfect as the stream,
You do your paddle-journey on.

And when you finally reach the sea,
Your journey still will not be done.
You'll take a look around and say,
"Good heavens, I guess I've just begun!"

By Ron Broomell

(Helen had always claimed she was related to loons—perhaps because loons are independent birds that are a little bit quirky?)

One Final Story

THIS BOOK HAS INCLUDED MANY STORIES AND QUOTES THAT have attempted to show bits and pieces of the "essence of Helen." I end it with a quote from Helen, provided by her friend Bev, that epitomizes who Helen was.

Bev and her husband John had taken Helen out to lunch. When Helen (who by then had a full set of dentures) ordered a grilled cheese sandwich, they suggested she order a steak instead. She answered, "I don't taste anything anyway, so I find it best to order a grilled cheese sandwich every time." Bev replied," That must be terrible, not to be able to taste anything." Helen's comment: "It would be if I let it."

Helen never let anything make her life terrible—not the loss of her mother at a very young age, not her marriage to a verbally abusive alcoholic, not her bad luck with romantic relationships after her divorce, not losing her house and all her belongings to a fire, not even Alzheimer's disease. She just wouldn't let anything disturb the life she wanted to lead.

It was a helluva life.

Timeline

(Some years are reconstructed guesses)

Roots

1874	John Perley Sprague born in Easton, Maine
1904	Married Mertie Belle Maxim in South Paris, Maine
1905	Camp Minocqua established
1905	Grace Maxim Sprague born in Chicago, Illinois
1912	Pottawattomie Lodge established

Growing up in a Summer Resort

1916	Helen Estes Sprague born in Grinnell, Iowa
1927	Mertie Maxim Sprague died in Minocqua, Wisconsin
1927-28	Attended Camp Warwick Woods in Sayner, Wisconsin

Teenager

1929-30	Attended the Holiday Camps in Hackensack, Minnesota
1930-31	Attended private school in Mississippi
1931	John P. Sprague married Sara Gregg Holiday in Hackensack, Minnesota
1931-32	Attended Evanston High School
1932-33	Attended Minocqua High School
1933	Clearwater Camp established
1933-34	Attended Evanston High School

1934-35	Attended Stevens College in Columbia, Missouri
1935-36	Attended Northwestern University in Evanston, Illinois
1936	Married John Graham Broomell in Ironwood, Michigan

Young Mother

1937	Graham Dare Broomell born in Evanston, Illinois
1938	Suzanne Sprague Broomell born in Evanston, Illinois
1941	Moved to Park Ridge, Illinois
1944	Moved to Elgin, Illinois
1946	Kenneth Foster Broomell born in Rhinelander, Wisconsin
1948	Ronald Holiday Broomell born in Elgin, Illinois

Return to the North Woods

1948	Moved to Minocqua
1949	Moved into own home
1959	Ann Dart Broomell born in Rhinelander, Wisconsin
1960	John P. Sprague died in Orlando, Florida
1961	Jennie Silver Broomell born in Rhinelander, Wisconsin
1962	Boundary Waters canoe trip with former Camp Minocqua campers and counselors, and three-year-old daughter Ann
1967	Divorced Jack

Free at Last

1963-73	Multiple Canadian wilderness canoe trips
1970s	Organized group wilderness trips (hiking/ backpacking trips, Sierra Club)
1973	Camp Minocqua closed

A Tripping Grandmother

1977	Three weeks on the Churchill River (northern Saskatchewan) with a companion
1979	Hitchhiked to Florida
	New Brunswick/Allagash canoe/hiking trip
1980	Outward Bound wilderness course
1981	First Yukon River trip
1983	Second Yukon River trip
1984	Backup for Verlen Kruger and Valerie Fons on Mississippi River Eddie Bauer Challenge
1985	Third Alaskan trip
1987	Fourth Alaskan trip
1988	House burned; remodeled and moved into the Pines
1989	Fifth Alaskan trip
1991	Last Alaskan trip

Old Age

1995	Diagnosed with Alzheimer's; moved to assisted living facility
1996	Moved into Alzheimer's unit
1998	Died at Rhinelander, Wisconsin

The inscription on Helen's memorial rock, located on the shore of Tomahawk Lake, says:

"COME SIT WITH ME"
IN LOVING TRIBUTE TO
HELEN SPRAGUE BROOMELL
DEC. 31, 1916 – MAR. 15, 1998
FEARLESS ADVENTURER AND BLITHE SPIRIT
"WELL, OF COURSE!"

Both of Helen's books *(Solo on the Yukon* and *Solo on the Yukon Again)* are out of print, but copies can sometimes be obtained on eBay or through Amazon's used booksellers. A limited number of copies are available from Dare Broomell, and I am working on republishing both books—check lulu.com or amazon.com for availability.